THE
PHILOSOPHY OF WAR

TEACHINGS OF
THE ORDER OF CHRISTIAN MYSTICS

THE PHILOSOPHY OF WAR

Teachings of The Order of Christian Mystics
The "Curtiss Books" freely available at
www.orderofchristianmystics.co.za

1. The Voice of Isis
2. The Message of Aquaria
3. The Inner Radiance
4. Realms of the Living Dead
5. Coming World Changes
6. The Key to the Universe
7. The Key of Destiny
8. Letters from the Teacher Volume I
9. Letters from the Teacher Volume II
10. The Truth about Evolution and the Bible
11. The Philosophy of War
12. Personal Survival
13. The Pattern Life
14. Four-Fold Health
15. Vitamins
16. Why Are We Here?
17. Reincarnation
18. For Young Souls
19. Gems of Mysticism
20. The Temple of Silence
21. The Divine Mother
22. The Soundless Sound
23. The Mystic Life
24. The Love of Rabiacca
25. Potent Prayers

Supporting Volumes

26. The Seventh Seal
27. Towards the Light

THE PHILOSOPHY
OF
WAR

Transcribed by
HARRIETTE AUGUSTA CURTISS
and
F. HOMER CURTISS, B.S., M.D.
Founders of
THE ORDER OF CHRISTIAN MYSTICS
and
AUTHORS OF THE "CURTISS BOOKS"

2014 EDITION

REPUBLISHED FOR THE ORDER BY
MOUNT LINDEN PUBLISHING
JOHANNESBURG, SOUTH AFRICA
ISBN: 978-1-920483-25-8

"Ministers of Christ and Stewards of the Mysteries of God."
1 Corinthians 4 vs. 1

COPYRIGHT 2014

BY
MOUNT LINDEN PUBLISHING

First Published in 1917

May be used for non-commercial, personal, research and educational use.
ALL RIGHTS RESERVED

PREFACE TO THE THIRD EDITION

After a period of twenty-two years since the *first edition*, we have been strongly urged to reissue this volume. One reason for this is that the outbreak of the war in Europe makes it as timely now as it was when the *first edition* was issued during the last World War.

Another reason is that we wish to make available to the younger generation our Cosmic Soul Science interpretation of the basic causes of all war, which proved so enlightening, helpful and comforting to the thousands of readers of the previous editions.

Since the principles remain the same and world conditions are so similar to those of the last war, we present this new *third edition* almost as it was first written—excepting the first two chapters—and with no attempt to bring it "up to date." For the applications of the law are as evident now as in the past.

We leave the text with only minor revisions and rearrangement of paragraphs because of the many statements whose later fulfillment makes them almost prophetic.

Our endeavor has always been to point out the folly of war, your personal responsibility in helping to produce the basic causes, and what positive and effective action you can take to counteract them and help to shorten these "days of tribulation." For if you all understand the workings of the law and courageously work with it, you can not only save yourself needless anxiety, fear and suffering, but you can also bring light and comfort to others, as well as "do your bit" to help stop the war.

F. Homer Curtiss, M.D.

Washington, D. C
September 12th, 1939.

PREFACE TO SECOND EDITION

When Chapters VI and VII were first published (1909) as monthly lessons for the *Order of Christian Mystics* they were written for advanced students of Cosmic Soul Science who were familiar with the fundamental terms and conceptions of Christian Mysticism, but since their publication in book form as the First Edition of this work there has been such a demand from the general public for further explanation of the principles on which those chapters were based, that three new chapters of more general interest and not so deeply metaphysical, but relating to the war in Europe, have been added. It is the prayer of the authors that the book thus enlarged may fulfil a still greater mission than the First Edition.

THE AUTHORS.

Philadelphia, Pa.,
June 1, 1918.

TABLE OF CONTENTS

CHAPTER		PAGE
	Preface to the Third Edition.	.v
	Preface to the Second Edition.	.vii
I	A Spiritual War Bulletin.	.1
II	World Peace.	.6
III	Why War?.	.8
IV	Various Aspects of War.	.32
V	Permanent Peace; God's Plan.	.57
VI	"The War" or the Principle of Resistance. .	.75
VII	The Battle of Armageddon.	.97
VIII	A World-Wide Call to Prayer.	.125
IX	A Prayer for World Harmony.	.141
X	The Symbology of the Stars and Stripes. .	.155

CHAPTER I

COPY OF A LETTER ISSUED BY

The Universal Religious Foundation, Inc.

A non-sectarian, non-profit, co-operative religious and philanthropic association incorporated for the purpose of promoting better understanding, fellowship and co-operation among the religions and peoples of the world.

INTERNATIONAL HEADQUARTERS
3516 QUEBEC STREET
WASHINGTON, D. C.
September 7th 1939.

A Spiritual War Bulletin

Danzig Not the Issue:

The war that has now begun in Europe is fundamentally not merely for the possession of Danzig and the Corridor. It is not merely to add Poland to the countries which Hitler—not the German people—has seized. It is not merely a war for the destruction of all political, economic, mental and spiritual freedom and self-determination, which are the basic ideals of the democracies. It is not even merely a war to impose a non-benevolent despotism upon free peoples. It is something far more fundamental and important.

Christianity or Atheism:

Behind all the outer reasons, it is a war for the ultimate destruction of Christianity and the type of civilization which Christianity has built up. It is fundamentally a war between the forces of the Anti-Christ[1] and those of the Christ: between the forces of darkness (the Black Forces) and the forces of Light; for only by the total destruction of all freedom of religious thought and ideals, and the complete domination of atheism, can dictator-despotisms be maintained.

---

[1] Please keep in mind tint the term "the Christ" or "the Christ-force," as used in the teachings of our Cosmic Soul Science, refer not to any personality, but to the Cosmic Christ-principle. This is the universal Life-aspect, the Creative-aspect, the spiritual Sun-aspect or the Son-aspect of the Trinity. The Father-force manifests as Divine Will, the Mother-force as Divine Love, while the Son-force or Christ-force manifests as the warm, loving Spiritual Life-force of all mankind, just as the physical Sun is the source of the warm, loving physical life-force of all the kingdoms of Nature, no matter what name may be given to this Cosmic Life-principle in other religions. It was this Cosmic Christ-principle which the Master Jesus embodied to a superlative degree.

The Anti-Christ is naturally made up of all the forces that oppose and work against the reign of the Christ in the hearts and minds of men.

No Personal Neutrality:

No matter what nations as a whole may do, once this fundamental truth is understood, there can be no personal neutrality. All honest thinkers must be on the side of religion in some form, and its spiritual ideals, or on the side of atheistic Bolshevism, despotism and the Anti-Christ.

Prepare to Sacrifice:

Your first duty, therefore, as a self-respecting free moral agent, is to search your mind and heart and *determine where you stand*. To what kind of civilization are you willing to submit and give your support? Once having chosen the side of spiritual freedom and independence, you must prepare to make any and every sacrifice,—personal, mental, financial,—as do the Communists, to protect, support, and spread the ideals you have chosen, through whatever channel or organization you may choose that most appeals to you for the expression of those ideals.

Pity, Not Hate:

Be sure not to hate, but to pity and to pray for the kindly but deceived and misled German people, for *it is not they who desire war*, but their leaders, who are obsessed by the black forces of the Anti-Christ.[1]

Radiate Strength:

You should cast out all fear, and remain calm centers of peace, poise, and radiant confidence, which you will unconsciously broadcast to all you contact. Be strong that others may find strength in your strength, and peace in your peace. Rely on the spiritual power of united, concentrated and consecrated prayer to free and to change the minds and hearts of the German people so that they will refuse to endure the continuation of war.

Loss of Morale:

The last war was stopped, not by lack of men and munitions but by the psychological and spiritual power of the millions who were praying for peace, which caused a "loss of morale" among the German people. And if this war is not suddenly stopped by revolution, cataclysm, or other tragedy, *it can be stopped* by the same force of prayer, producing another "loss of morale."

---

[1] As explained in subsequent chapters herein.

Pray at Noon:

We therefore invite all who will enlist under the White Banner of the Christ to join with us each day at noon or oftener in a "Prayer for World Harmony" and a "Prayer for World Peace" to help us mobilize the world for peace. Free copies of these prayers will be sent to anyone upon request. (Please enclose postage.)

Sincerely yours, for Peace, Harmony
and Brotherhood,
F. HOMER CURTISS, M.D.
President

CHAPTER II

WORLD PEACE[1]

"To whom shall I speak, and give warning, that they may hear? Behold, their ear is uncircumcised, and they cannot harken: behold the word of the Lord is unto them a reproach; they have no delight in it."
Jeremiah, VI, 10.

"Men's hearts failing them for fear, and for looking after those things which are coming upon the earth.... And when these things begin to come to pass, then look up, and lift up your heads; for your redemption draweth nigh."
St. Luke, XXI, 26-8.

"I will pray with the Spirit, and I will pray with understanding."
I Corinthians, XIV, 15.

Stability Essential:

Once we have a clear realization of the fundamental laws back of world conditions today, then we can decide what is our individual duty in regard to them.

All living and growing things require certain basic stabilized conditions for their perfect manifestation. The grain requires the stable conditions of the furrow, the flower the garden, the egg the nest, the babe the home, the nation

---

[1] Released Sept. 7, 1939.

its homeland, as the field for its expression. While activities and changes are necessary within these stabilized conditions *e. g.*, plants need cultivating, eggs need turning, children need training, nations need governing, etc.—nevertheless, a general condition of peace—of uninterrupted constructive activities—is essential for development, maturity and perfection. Therefore, *permanent peace is God's plan* for His various manifestations in the world. Hence it is man's ultimate destiny.

Man's Responsibility:

But because man has free-will to follow the desires of the flesh and of his own petty personality, instead of working in harmony with God's Divine Plan, he sets up antagonisms and destructive forces between himself and God and between himself and his fellow men, both personally and nationally. These destructive forces naturally revert to man—their creator—to be adjusted and redeemed, or to be experienced by him, personally perhaps in fist-fights or other disastrous conditions, and nationally as wars.

Not the Father's Will:

The terrible conditions that prevail today are, therefore, *not the Father's will*, but are the wilfull creations of man; the result of his opposition to Divine Will and his violation of Divine Law. Furthermore, the unbrotherliness, intolerance, selfishness, greed and aggression now manifesting are not entirely the creations of the present generation, but are the accumulations of all mankind which were not worked out through the last World War and otherwise, which must still come up for adjustment.

The Basic Causes:

These inharmonies find expression not directly through the masses of the people themselves, but through leaders whose ideals are at variance with the laws of God and His Divine Plan. The *basic causes* of these conditions, therefore, are first, ignorance of our origin and destiny, and second, our lack of response to our inner God-guidance, our turning away from religion, our lack of recognition of our relation to God, and our failure to correlate with and worship Him.

The Anti-Christ:

This failure of proper religious training and practice is augmented by a deliberate campaign by the forces of the Anti-Christ to enslave the nations of the world, both by stimulating the ignoble animal passions of selfishness, greed and national aggrandizement, and by a revolt against all forms of religion and worship of God. The conflict, then, is not primarily against men and economic and other material conditions, but against the "principalities and powers of darkness" which seek to ruin all forms of religion, law and order, and finally all the peace, culture and beauties that man's slow evolution from barbarism to civilization has won for him.

Anti-religious Propaganda:

Perhaps the most notable instrument to be obsessed by the dark forces was the monk Rasputin. Through him the evil forces began to infect and demoralize Russia. But the full fury of the destructive forces found expression through the World War. Yet, since the forces of right, justice, freedom and independence won that war, the Anti-Christ had to fall back upon fostering irreligion, thus winning Russia definitely over to anti-religion. And it is that virus that has more or less infected the nations of Europe, and has even found some foothold in the Western world. And since no nation can follow the principles of love, tolerance, freedom and independence of the individual as inculcated by Christianity and at the same time engage in wars of aggression and national aggrandizement, *the fundamental conflict is between Christianity on the one hand and Paganism on the other*; between the followers of the Christ and those of the Anti-Christ.

What to Do:

What can you as an individual do about it? The first step is to realize that God's plan is for permanent peace, and determine to *adjust your personal life to it*. For only as you bring your heart and mind and life into harmony with God's plan for peace, can you manifest mental, emotional and bodily harmony. And there can be no permanent peace or harmony among nations without the expression of peace and harmony *within the individuals* of the nations. The first step, therefore, is to establish permanent peace and harmony *in your own life*.

Your Reaction:

If you find this attainment more difficult now than formerly; if you are more nervous, more irritable, more selfish than usual, when you have eliminated all possible physical causes, then look for a metaphysical cause. Realize that the terrible inharmonies engendered by warring ideologies and warring nations have caused the accumulation of vast clouds of destructive forces which are broadcast throughout the mental atmosphere of all humanity. Hence, every time you give way to anger, intolerance, antagonism or other destructive emotions, even impatience and irritation, you open the door of your mind and tune-in to the black clouds of antagonism generated by the race. If they are thus admitted, through even a crack, their antagonism may flow in with ever increasing power until you are swept away into an outburst of passion which you had no intention of expressing and which may greatly surprise and mortify you. In this way *you are personally contributing* to the forces which culminate in war. Therefore *watch your reactions* and control them.

Your Responsibility:

Since "thoughts are things" and words are their avenue of expression, every time you talk of, or excuse or palliate war you are adding to the forces of war. And every time you neglect an opportunity to speak for, pray for, and radiate peace, harmony and love, *you have failed in your duty*, and to that extent *you are personally responsible* for the continuation of the war-spirit. Do you choose to have such a reproach rest upon your conscience? Therefore, every time you feel inharmony arising, *instantly check yourself* and *refuse to respond to it*, and counteract it by concentrating on *feeling* and positively *radiating* peace and love. Instead of responding, smile and say; "Thy banner over me, O God, is peace, harmony and love. It penetrates me, fills me, radiates from me and blesses all I contact."

The Next Step:

Having polarized yourself to positive peace radiations, the next step is to do your part to neutralize, counteract and dissipate the destructive thought-forces in the world at large which make for war, by consciously broadcasting their opposites. Since the World War was stopped, not by a lack of men and munitions, but by psychological and spiritual forces—thoughts and prayers—which caused a "loss of morale" in the ranks and in the homes of the Central Powers, and which made the call for an armistice imperative, just so can the present war-thoughts be neutralized by the same means.

And the greatest psychological and spiritual instrument to that end is earnest and understanding prayer.

The Power of Prayer:

We therefore earnestly urge all who wish thus to enlist their forces on the side of peace, freedom and righteousness, to repeat some such prayer as our *Prayer for World Peace* or our *Prayer for World Harmony*,[1] morning, noon and night, but *especially at noon*, and spread the ideal as widely as possible that its spiritual vibrations may affect and inspire the hearts of all mankind, and particularly the leaders of nations, with its ideals, thus dissolving all thoughts of aggression, domination and war.

Principles, Not Personalities:

Systematically spread the thought that it is wrong principles, ideals and rules of life that you must combat, rather than persons or peoples, however misguided they may seem to you. The masses express largely what they are taught. Therefore, *do not condemn any person or nation, nor despise any religion or race.* They may sincerely believe what they have been

---
[1] See Charter IX.

taught is right, no matter how ignorant they are of God's law of permanent peace, or how much they have been misled. Simply envelop all who hold negative and inharmonious ideals of domination and aggression, and neutralize all destructive forces, with the radiance of Divine Light, Life and Love.

Concentration:

As we said in our *Prayer for World Harmony* in 1917; "The concentration of the minds and hearts of thousands of advanced students in many lands who understand the power and reality of the currents of force generated by thought, aspiration, love, prayer and the will-for-righteousness, will cause such an outpouring of creative thought-force and love-force that it will rise like incense into the higher realms and rain down upon the hearts and minds of humanity with such quickening power as to fructify every mind capable of grasping and responding to the ideals which the prayer embodies, and vivify them into action.[1]

You Are an Important Factor:

The results must be gained, not by an arbitrary Being who imposes His will upon a help-

---

[1] *Coming World Changes*, Curtiss, 115.

less humanity, but by your responding to the guidance of His love and compassion within yourself. Hence there is not a single man, woman or child who cannot be *an active factor* in bringing "peace on earth, good will toward men." For by understanding the law you can consciously focus the power of Spirit like a blow-torch to melt and dissolve all obstructing conditions. Thus will you become one of His peacemakers.

Spiritual Fire:

Realize that when prayers are thus consciously and understandingly used, they are not mere pious words, but form definite channels through which spiritual fire can be invoked and focused upon humanity. With this God-power ever at hand waiting to be invoked and used, we must not ask God to save humanity while humanity makes no effort; for it is humanity which must save itself by learning to use the powers God has already given it. And the first to use these powers should be all advanced thinkers who can understand the law. And those who realize the power of prayer are responsible for its use.

Prayer at Noon:

Since it is noon somewhere every minute of the twenty four hours, the concentration of thousands of hearts and minds at that hour will generate a mighty current of spiritual force of great dynamic power which will sweep continuously around the world night and day. Consciously flood the minds of all mankind with the realization that only through physical, mental and spiritual freedom can the highest aspirations of their Souls and the greatness of their nations be attained. For all must realize that not by force and compulsion, but by peace, reconciliation,[1] brotherhood and cooperation can the prosperity, culture and happiness of all peoples be achieved.

Prayer for World Peace

O Thou glorious Source of all life, light and love, our Lord God almighty! from whose heart the Ray of Spirit in each mortal is sprung! let the realisation of our oneness in Thee descend upon our hearts as heavenly dew, refreshing our souls.

May the love of God and the fellowship of all mankind—without regard to race, creed or con-

---

[1] See lesson *Reconciliation*, Curtiss.

dition—so fill our hearts and minds that each will gladly unite his forces for the attainment of peace, fellowship and co-operation.

May all persons and classes and nations cease their conflicts, and unselfishly strive for peace and good-will, that world peace may speedily be attained.

Let the calm of Thy eternal peace, which passeth all intellectual understanding, envelop us with its divine serenity. May it quiet the turmoil of our minds, and the conflict of our desires, dissolve our fears, and reveal to us the essential brotherhood of all mankind.

Thus shall the power of Thy loving Spirit bring victory over all opposition to the establishment of Thy peace on earth, and good-will among mankind. Amen.

Pause after each sentence and meditate upon it. Visualize its radiance going out to envelop all mankind. See the radiance which this Prayer invokes dispelling the dark clouds of inharmony and war as the Sun dispels fog, and stimulating the growth of the good in each heart as the Sun stimulates the growth of the sprout when the fog has been dispelled and the Sun can perform its constructive work. Thus will you do your part to manifest God's plan for world peace.

CHAPTER III

WHY WAR?[1]

> "The world is a field of battle where liberty struggles with inertia by the opposition of active force."
> *Transcendental Magic*, Lévi, 31.

Why War?

The chaotic conditions now existing in Europe have elicited many questions from our students throughout the world, especially those in European countries, as to the mystical meaning and the philosophical reason for the apparent necessity for war, and *why it is permitted* by a God of Love and Wisdom. In other words, what is the reason for and the place of war in the Cosmic Scheme or the Grand Plan of the Universe? This chapter is an attempt, in a few paragraphs, merely to outline and make comprehensible a stupendous subject whose roots go deep into the beginnings of manifestation, and which would require a large volume properly to

---

[1] Altho this was released on Oct. 7th, 1914, it is still singularly appropriate in 1939.

elucidate. For the principle of war is an expression of cosmic law.

National Sickness:

Strife and war among nations are simply evidences of inharmony and sickness in the body of humanity; an effort of the body politic to slough off those atoms which refuse to respond to the higher key-note of civilization that is struck by the more advanced conceptions of Harmony, Brotherhood and Cooperation among nations.[1]

War a Lancet:

War may be likened to the cruel lancet of the surgeon which opens a festering boil. It causes temporary suffering and bloodshed, but it permits the escape of the mass of inharmony and corruption which, if not otherwise neutralized, would poison the entire body. And no real healing can take place until the focus of infection is utterly wiped out.

Your Battles:

In the daily battles for poise, control and harmony which you begin consciously to fight

---

[1] The atoms thus sloughed off are not only the individual lives sacrificed in war, but are also the false ideals of selfish isolation and individual aggrandizement regardless of others, that obstruct the upward evolution of humanity as a whole.

as soon as you endeavor to follow a higher ideal, you may possibly find yourself worsted in some of the skirmishes of the early stages. And evil and inharmony may accumulate until it can no longer be held back and must find physical expression.

Thoughts Will Express:

It is a well-known principle of psychology that thoughts express themselves through their creators in terms of action, unless counteracted by opposite thoughts of greater power. But no matter how many skirmishes are lost, if you persistently follow the Light of your highest Ideal, be it ever so primitive to others, it will lead you step by step to ultimate victory. If you find yourself facing such an outbreak, it means that you have created more inharmony or evil than your present stage of spiritual unfoldment is able to transmute, hence the precipitation.

Light Wins:

In *all wars*, on every plane of manifestation, the forces which represent the Light; which fight for progress, enlightenment, civilization, the Brotherhood of Man and of Nations: which truly fight on the side of St. George against the Dragon, *must ultimately win*, for they become channels through which the constructive, uplifting and spiritualizing currents of the Cosmic Forces can find expression and manifest on earth.

As we have said elsewhere, before any cycle can close and the cycle return to its primordial state of equilibrium, everything that persistently stands in the way and prevents the manifestation of Divine Will, or the Ideal of that particular cycle; *everything that resists* the indrawal and union; that refuses to respond to the higher vibration or key-note of that cycle, in other words, which refuses to be redeemed, *must* be wiped out of the path of that closing cycle and make way for the manifestation of the new.

Adjustment Necessary:

Therefore *there must be* a great adjustment at the close of *every* cycle,—and we are now living in the days when the old Piscean Age is still overlapping the beginning of the Aquarian Age of Brotherhood—whether it be of Race, sub-race, nation or individual. If the cycle is sufficiently advanced to permit the adjustment to be made by responding to the Law of Harmony expressed through Love, Tolerance, Brotherhood and Unselfishness—whether of individuals, nations or Races—then there need be no war, for the *resistance* has been overcome.

Precipitated Evil:

But if *the resistance to the Divine* has built up such a mass of inharmony (evil) that the spiritual force of that cycle is not sufficient to redeem it, then the adjustment must come as a physical precipitation of the stored up inharmony, through the avenue of physical conflict or war; just as a cloud which is so saturated with moisture that the Sun cannot absorb (redeem) it, must be precipitated as rain, hail or snow ere the light of the Sun can manifest on earth.

Baptism of Blood:

As we said in 1917:[1] "The countries of Europe, each under its own banner, have been passing through their baptism of blood and then purification by fire; for only thus can their sins be washed away and their chaff and evil weeds consumed. America must also lift high her

---
[1] *The Sign Aquarius*, Curtiss.

banner and take her place in the purifying fire ere the mystical 'twelve thousand' of her tribe can be chosen and sealed. Only those who endure to the end receive the blessing. For out of this terrible baptism there shall arise a purified humanity."

France in War:

"France has had many baptismal experiences, and each time she has taken an onward step, but her natural frivolous disposition has always prevented her from taking the great step which she some day must take – *i.e.*, the recognition of the Divine Law and its guiding power in her affairs as a nation. For she rightfully belongs in the van of those countries which are ready to embrace this newest, truest, yet oldest of all presentations of the Wisdom Religion.

Her Opportunity:

"Therefore France is once again having her opportunity to learn of the inner realities of life and be willing to follow them. This we hope she is learning today through her terrible baptism of blood and her blinding tears of repentance. And we already see in her eyes the deep comprehension and the steadfast determination of one who knows. Will she remain true to her vision?

England's Tenacity:

"England is also passing through the greatest testing in her history, but there are certain racial (tribal) characteristics which make her lessons hard to learn. She can stand up with bulldog tenacity for truth and right as she sees it, yet with the same tenacity she holds on to old ideas and conceptions and traditions, and finds it hard to let them go and admit that there can be any new interpretation of truth.[1] This fault has heretofore always kept her just a little behind in the great march of spiritual evolution.

Australia:

"Therefore we will consider her in the person of her eldest son and heir, Australia. Here we have a virgin country, unsullied by war; English, yet not England; the oldest land upon the globe; a country that carries within its bosom the magnetic influences of Those who first gave to this world its impetus; of Those who first

---

[1] Since this was written in 1917 she has learned many of her lessons and made radical changes in her national life. Capable observers have written that there has been a radical change in the characteristics of her people toward sympathy, tenderness and brotherhood.

descended and touched the children of men with the divine spark of spiritual intelligence.[1] It now lies in a great measure uncultivated and dormant, with large areas entirely barren. Her cry comes to us out of the dim, forgotten past. Her possibilities are great, but will her children awaken? Will she lift high the banner of her tribe and fall in line with the others?

Russia:

"Russia is a mere child among the nations, just emerging into adolescence. She has passed her childhood stage of crudity and irresponsible cruelty and is now facing the temptations of youth. But as she wakes up in this great day of trial she begins to feel the sinews of manhood struggling for expression. When this great nation finds herself, as she is sure to do sooner or later, the war will quickly end.

Her Awakening:

"She is now passing through a crucial test, like a giant awakening from slumber and finding himself in peril. She is beginning to open her eyes, although they are still clouded and heavy with sleep. Reality and unreality merge

---

[1] See *The Voice of Isis*, Curtiss, Chapter XIII.

into each other. She has had many lurid dreams. She has ascended several rungs of the great ladder and has seen the angels descending. Will she let them enter in and purify her? Or will she let a youthful lust for blood and a desire for revenge pull her down?[1]

Germany:

"Germany we might call the bad boy of the tribes, altho now fully grown. Through ambition and pride he has opened the door to the hordes of evil forces which are seeking to obsess humanity and wreak their will upon it. Through giving expression to these forces, he has become the instrument through which they are being poured out into the world to the testing of the other nations, just as Judas became the instrument of testing to the other disciples.

Her Humiliation:

"Hence his days of testing are mighty and terrible on all planes. For Germany is not a child, but a full-grown man, knowing good from evil. He has chosen, therefore let us draw a

---

[1] Since this was written the effects of her great injustices and sufferings have brought on a fever of delirium which saps her strength and makes her see all things distorted, taking liberty to mean license, etc. She will recover, but as in all fevers, it will be followed by a period of extreme weakness.

veil over his ultimate sorrow and humiliation and pray that the time of his affliction may be shortened.

Lust for Power:

"The Germans, altho of age, have not yet reached the fulness of their national and personal karma; have not yet climbed to the top of the first mystic 'mount' which is Sinai in the wilderness, or the intellectual heights where the great mass of the nation have awakened to their individual responsibility. For they are still dominated by the lust for power, dominion and commercial supremacy, hence cannot see that material advance, when not accompanied with corresponding moral and spiritual advance, is an *ignis fatuus* leading them to destruction.

Military Apron-strings:

"Germany as a nation, although fully grown up and responsible, is still in leading strings. Like a young man who has reached his majority, yet who has never been permitted to go outside the front yard, it has not learned the lessons of life. It has never been permitted to exercise the rights or assume the responsibilities of manhood. It has always been told to do this or not to do that. It is still tied to the military apron strings of the Kaiser.[1]

Needs Leading:

"The majority of the individuals who make up its inhabitants are in a mental state in which they desire to be led rather than be held responsible for their actions. This has been repeatedly demonstrated by her soldiers on the battlefield, even by those drawn from the higher walks of life. They therefore do not demand anything higher of their Kaiser[1] than such leadership as will bring material success, no matter what the price, hence they are not ready for anything better. And therefore it would be cruel to demand that as a nation it should face the responsibilities of a manhood it has never been permitted to develop, although that great lesson must be learned quickly.

Learning Lessons:

"However, many are waking up, only to find themselves led by the leash they themselves have accepted and made possible. They must therefore be let alone to *learn the lessons which servitude and failure alone can teach.* To bring

---
[1] Today Hitler.

upon them wholesale cataclysms and disasters of nature before these lessons are learned would not fulfil their just karma.

Their Karma:

"They must be allowed to eat to their fill of the fruit they themselves have picked, *i.e.*, their belief in the wisdom and justice of the leadership of the Kaiser [1] and his policies. So will they find out the bitterness of the fruits he obtains for them, thus proving in the only way that they will realize and accept, his inability to deliver that which he has promised and taught them was the greatest good and the highest end, ere they are ready for anything higher. When they do awaken and begin to learn their lesson, then as a nation they will begin to reap the terrible national karma they have created by blindly following the Kaiser.[1] But until they are ready to realize and understand and learn their lesson the Great Law must take its course.

Russia's Karma:

"They will have plenty of karma when their day of reaping begins, just as Russia is today reaping the national karma which as a nation

---

[1] Today Hitler.

she created by her abject submission to the ignominy of slavery and Czarism. For while it seems as though Russia's recent actions are the result of childish and *almost insane folly*, nevertheless they spring from the same trait which permitted them to submit tamely for so many generations to the shackles, the knout and the unspeakable degradation of Siberia.

Your Duty:

"There are many other nations of whom you would scarcely think, who are bearing their banners and passing their testings. Therefore do not give too great heed when you hear that America is to be the seat of the New Race or that any special part of the United States has been chosen for its center. For all the nations and tribes are in the melting-pot, and *the one whose people come forth most fitted* will be the one chosen.

Respond Gladly:

"It is man, therefore, responding of his own free-will to the guidance of the Divine, and not the dictates of an arbitrary Being who imposes his Will upon a helpless humanity, who must bring about 'Peace on earth, good will toward men.' Hence there is not a single man or woman who cannot be an active factor in bringing the Golden Age of Love, Peace, Harmony and Brotherhood into manifestation the sooner, through the controlling of thoughts, words and emotions, and by *overcoming his or her resistance*, and responding more and more understandingly and gladly, to the upward urge of the Divine."

From *The Sign Aquarius*, The Twelve Tribes (Released March 7, 1917).

CHAPTER IV

VARIOUS ASPECTS OF WAR

Extracts culled from the authors' other writings concerning war.

Federation of Nations:

While this present conflict seems wholly evil, it is not entirely so for the Race. Not only will the old karmic debts be adjusted, but the contending nations will be allowed to enter into a federation in which the independence of each nation or people will be guaranteed—as brothers, some older, some younger—in the great social family. Thus war will be prevented for a long period, and we can enter a new era with a clean slate, as it were.

War Develops Unselfishness:

The war is developing in the Race as a whole, an enormous number of the feminine qualities—love, compassion, sympathy, devotion, unselfishness and service—so necessary as the Race enters the Aquarian or Woman's Age,[1] the sign of the Son of Man in the heavens.

Advanced Nations:

Among the contending nations the English, French and Germans have reached the zenith of their cycles as nations and hence must be tested ere they can enter the new cycle.[2] They are classed among the nations which represent the highest stage of civilization, culture, intellectual and material advance on the planet today, but they must now prove the truth of their proud boasts; must prove whether their civilization and culture is the result of true spiritual growth or whether it is the mere veneer of intellectual and material attainment, founded in cruelty and intolerance, and without corresponding spiritual unfoldment.

A Spiritual Basis:

Has their so-called advance in civilization brought their people into a greater realization of the *spiritual basis* of all manifestation? Has

---

[1] See chapter on The Woman's Age" in *Why Are We Here?* Curtiss.
[2] Since the above was first published America entered the war as a full-grown youth now assuming the great responsibilities of manhood. Hence America and her institutions had also to be tested and proved by fire.

it led them to strive for a more conscious communion with the realms of spiritual consciousness as a daily personal experience?

Soul Craving:

Has it taught them the folly of seeking to satisfy the ceaseless craving of the Soul for *union with its Source*, through the gratification of the senses or the possession of material things?

Law of Brotherhood:

Has their scientific study of the wonderful cooperation and brotherhood existing among the cells, tissues and organs of every unit of organic life led them—if for no other reason, as a matter of efficiency—to follow *the same law* and express greater tolerance, cooperation and brotherhood among themselves as members of the body of humanity?

The Position of Woman:

Have their studies led them to recognize the true position of woman as the Priestess of the Household, the complement and co-worker with man; the spiritual head of the family, as man is the material; the inspirer and leader in all spiritual, ethical and moral problems?

Emergency Tests:

In time of emergency, stress and strain, when there is scarcely time for thought, will the culture of these nations enable them instinctively to display more love, compassion, self-sacrifice and humanity—simply because man is man—than the less cultured nations would under similar conditions? Or will they relapse to the level of the uncultured animal man who fights solely for self?

Test of Civilization:

This is the test which their civilization must stand. And those nations which show most conclusively that these higher qualities have been built into their national consciousness must be the ones to dominate and manifest these qualities more perfectly in the world's arena during the coming cycle of the New Age.

Slavonic Nations:

The Slavonic nations, on the other hand, have not reached the zenith of their evolution, but are on the upward arc. Hence the more primitive qualities of their civilization may be used by the Great Law as instruments with which to accomplish the testing of the more advanced, and to make possible the inauguration of the New Era.

Period of Revolt:

When the physical conflict is over a terrible mental revolt against all forms of restraint, both in government and religion, will burst forth.[1] It will be a period of extremes, extremes of individualism; a period when the opposition against all systematized or organized spiritual teachings, which is even now manifesting under various doctrines of religious and so-called "soul freedom," will find extreme expression.

Agnosticism:

It will be a period both of extreme agnosticism and extreme individualistic teaching, when any fantastic theory, even without a rational or philosophic basis, will find a hearing and followers. At the same time there will be a strong feeling upon the part of those who cling to the old conceptions that it is their duty to humanity to enforce the old religious ideals.

---

[1] Since this was first published (1914) it has already begun its fulfillment through the action of the Communists, but they will not be the only ones.

Religions Tolerance:

This will be a great test as to whether religious intolerance has been outgrown;[1] for there can be no permanent peace until the minds of a majority of mankind have been sufficiently developed, broadened and spiritualized to banish it forever.

War of Ideologies:

Hence all churches, orders, movements and societies professing a spiritual basis will on the one hand have radicals whose extremes will bring them into disrepute, while on the other hand they will have those who will laugh at, ridicule, discredit, oppose and persecute them. And the same fire that has manifested as physical war will again sweep the world as a mental, spiritual and psychic conflict. And it is always those nearest and dearest or those companions who helped us create the Karma, who are used by the Great Law to test us and adjust the Karma.

Beliefs Tested:

It will be a time when all spiritual movements will be under a cloud, when spiritually "The

---

[1] Years later this has been fulfilled by the treatment of the Jews by the dictators.

brother shall betray the brother to death, and the father the son: and children shall rise against their parents, and shall cause them to be put to death." Therefore it will be a period of great testing; a period when every heart who has realized the reality of the spiritual world and its forces must be securely grounded in the philosophy and stand firmly and unshakably for his or her beliefs, even though to do so involves ridicule, persecution and mental suffering. For every system of teaching not founded upon the rock of divine reality and expressed in terms suitable to the new conditions must pass away to make room for the new.

The Elect:

These conditions will be so terrible that they will last only a very few years, for we are told that "for the elect's sake those days shall be shortened. . . . And except those days should be shortened, there should be no flesh saved." The only way that the "elect" can prove themselves is by their sincerity, their steadfastness, their trust and their determination to hold calmly to their spiritual ideals and to *rely absolutely upon their divine, inner guidance,* while they pray without ceasing that these days be shortened.

The Great Teacher:

Words and arguments will be of no avail. The truth of their beliefs can be proved only by *living* them. All such will be like bright and shining lights in this period of mental and spiritual darkness, or more correctly, blindness. It will be at the close of this period that the long expected Great Teacher, the Avatar, will appear to reassure distracted humanity of the *spiritual basis of all manifestation* and to outline a new and higher conception of the spiritual life and its forms of expression.[1]

Spiritual Flour:

"Today, by means of the horror and carnage of war, the Mills of the Gods are grinding the grains of spiritual attainment, disrupting the husks of prejudice, the hampering limitations of country and nation and Race; freeing the individual grains of tolerance, kindness, compassion, love, self-sacrifice, helpfulness and brotherhood from the personal limitations, and grind-

---

[1] (The above was released Sept. 15th, 1917.)

ing them all together into the flour from which, under the direction of the coming Great Teacher, the Bread of the New Age can be made.

Sundering Limitations:

"Not only is this true of those nations which are participating in the great conflict and bearing its burdens, but it is true in a lesser degree for all nations. For it needs just such worldhorrors as are transpiring today to break open the limiting shell of national consciousness and of separate organization, and awaken into activity those Souls who are the germ-centers or the individual grains from which the Bread of Life must be made. The storms of carnage and disaster are but the mill-wheels of the gods grinding the separate grains into homogeneous flour which the hand of the enlightened Christ-man must make into Bread for all the world.

Giant Weeds:

"Remember, the horrors of war are not a part of the Divine Plan; *they are created by man*. By its cruelty and inhumanity to man, by its unbrotherliness, intolerance—even among the enlightened. And by its trampling into the dust the small and seemingly insignificant independent germ-centers scattered among its millions, humanity has so hardened the husk of the Race-seed and so buried its vital germ-cells, in its wild rush for wealth, power, dominion and self-aggrandizement, that when 'the sign of the Son of Man'[1] arose in the heavens and began to pour out its cleansing and fertilizing power, the giant weeds of selfishness and antagonism sprang up and had to be let grow with the grain until the harvest time. And the weeds are now being destroyed that the golden grains may be ground into flour.

Husks of Personality:

"Woe, then, to those who, either individually or collectively, refuse to be garnered in; who refuse to place their golden grains of personal attainment, understanding and ability to help humanity, in the great Mill of the Gods and allow the outer husks of personal and limiting conceptions to be broken open and all their forces liberated, ground and unselfishly unified with others to make the nourishing Bread of Life which the power of the Cosmic Christ can

---

[1] The zodiacal sign Aquarius into which our solar system has just entered. For details see *The Message of Aquaria*, Curtiss.

bless and break and give to them to distribute to the multitude."

From *The Eucharist*, Part II, Symbol of the Bread (Released Oct. 7, 1916).

Blood-stained Path:

"Largely due to the materialization of spiritual symbols, the onward march of civilization proceeds along a path so stained with the blood of man that it is like a red, red river reaching back into the beginnings of the Race. The history of the Christian Church—which should be the Bride of the Christ, arrayed in garments of spotless white—began in bloodshed and ever since it has been one sickening story of the blood of man shed by his brother in the name of the Prince of Peace and the Lord of Love.

The Inquisition:

From the holocausts of the early- days in Rome, through the Inquisition, with its devilish devices for adding torture to the shedding of blood, through the exploitation of less powerful peoples by the more powerful in the name of Christianity, down to the present day when half the world is calling upon the same God for the

Various Aspects Of War 43

blood of its fellow-men, through all this the justification of blood sacrifice has held sway.

America's Guilt:

"Even our own United States, the so-called land of freedom, liberty and justice, was founded in bloodshed—with certain, shining exceptions such as the land *purchased* by William Penn, and the missions founded along the Pacific coast by the Franciscan fathers. When driven from the Old World by bloody persecutions in the name of religion, Christianity planted its standards in this New World *by the same methods.* And later on these same methods were continued in the burning of witches, and in the treatment of the slaves and the Indians.

America's Karma:

"As the days of reckoning and readjustment come, the days foretold by Jesus when we would see the sign Aquarius (Sign of the Son of Man) ruling in the heavens, as the celestial Waterbearer pours out in greater abundance the waters of life—the mother-aspect of the Cosmic Life-force—need we be surprised that the harvest in the Old World is one of bloodshed? Nor need we of America think that we can escape our ultimate baptism of blood during this great cyclic readjustment; for the Great Law will not hold us guiltless.

Wrong Thinking:

"Only by reaping the karmic result—not so much of the deeds of the flesh as of *the wrong thinking, the false teaching* and the materialization of the symbols of the "new testament"—can humanity learn to look beneath the surface, beneath the literal meaning of symbols and words and enter into the spirit of that which is intended.

Karma Is Readjustment:

"Karma is not so much reaping the results of past acts as it is *the readjustment of the effects of wrong thinking*. It is not "an eye for an eye and a tooth for a tooth/' but the equalization of conditions and the bringing about of exact justice. It is largely the suffering which logically results from wrong thinking, that brings to the world, as to the individual, an awakening in which it refuses to follow tradition and precedent when they no longer coincide with its enlightened conceptions of that which is best.

Wrong Interpretation:

"We of the New Day desire to obey the words of Jesus: 'Be ye therefore perfect/ and yet, as we look back over history we see that if the teaching that mankind can be saved only through a blood sacrifice has brought the world to such a pass, something must be radically wrong. And yet since the same symbols are found in all other religions and are world old, the source of the wrong must be sought not in the symbols themselves but in the orthodox and *materialized interpretation* of them.

War a Blood-sacrifice:

"For the world today is thoroughly convinced that war, which is but the ultimate of blood sacrifice, does not produce justice, does not bring perfection, does not tend to make all men brethren or all peoples children of the one loving Father who calls them to His table and breaks the Bread and passes the Cup and calls upon them to eat and drink unto everlasting life."

From *The Eucharist*, Symbol of the Blood (Released Nov. 7, 1916).

Karma in the Bible:

"Ever since the childhood of the Race, man has been disobedient to his Divine Guidance:

has been ambitious, selfish, cruel and bloodthirsty. Yet in spite of this, civilization has steadily advanced in a cyclic and spiral fashion. This has been accomplished through the Great Law constantly working with man in its sevenfold manner, always trying to inspire him with higher ideals, always utilizing for his learning, through the Law as Karma, the suffering he brings upon himself. This Law is enunciated in the *Bible* in the words: 'Whatsoever a man sow, that shall he also reap. . . . One jot or one tittle shall in nowise pass from the law, till all be fulfilled. . . . Inasmuch as ye have done it unto one of the least of these my brethren, ye have done it unto me.'

Oppression Forbidden:

"Through this law, which is divine Justice, man is taught through actual experience that he cannot love God and hate his brother; that he cannot truly worship God while he oppresses even the least of the ignorant little ones who are his brethren in Christ, without in some life, either now or in the future, himself suffering from injustice, hatred and oppression, until Saturn has gathered all the crop of unbrotherliness his heart has brought forth. And as with individuals, so with nations.

Divine Fruition:

"And after the reaping, when the golden grains have been gathered by the Four Winds from all the fields of earth—those who have come 'out of great tribulation' and whose garments have been made white 'in the blood of the Lamb'—then the mighty downpouring of the Water of Life will just as surely bring to fruition the seeds of man's divine nature as it already has the lower; those spiritual seeds which, 'sown in corruption; it is raised in incorruption; it is sown in dishonor; it is raised in glory: it is sown in weakness; it is raised in power: it is sown in a natural body; it is raised in a spiritual body.' For the world this new spiritual body will be the Aquarian Age, and for each individual a new conception of love, light, power and life; the actual unfolding of the Christ-consciousness and a manifestation of its power in the life.

Saturn the Reaper:

"But first there must come the realization that because Saturn must reap the tares you have sown he is not to be thought of as evil, but as one of the Sons of God[1] who in divine love and compassion clears the ground that you may bring forth the Christ-seed and reap your spiritual harvest.

Mercury and Venus:

And just as Saturn is an aspect of God, so also is Mercury, he who takes your every aspiration godward, your every effort toward victory and your every realization to the very throne of God. Then, through the intercession of this winged messenger, Venus or Divine Love enters and builds her nest in your heart and brings forth her young. As you thus become a real Aquarian, you will at last realize that because you have loved much, much has been forgiven."

From *The Sign Aquarius*, The New Age (Released Jan. 7, 1917).

Spiritual Grain:

"The whole world is today a great testing ground for a similar ingathering. It is the field and humanity is the grain. The angels are the reapers and the harvest time is now at hand. Out of all the grains that grow in the

---
[1] See *Job*, i. 6.

fields of earth, comparatively few are fitted and ready to be made into the Bread of Eternal Life. But it is just as possible, through the scientific application of the laws of growth, to double and treble the nutritive power of the spiritual grain as it is of the physical grain. By spreading the truths of man's spiritual heritage and the laws of his spiritual growth, mankind can consciously multiply the quantity, improve the quality and hasten the ripening of the spiritual grain.

Workers Needed:

"While the angels are the reapers, they need loving Souls on earth who are eager, devoted, trained and ready to go out into the fields and vineyards and bring the golden sheaves into the granary of the Lord. We, individually and collectively, who can recognize the times in which we live *and the great events foreshadowed in the heavens*, must work with all our hearts and minds and powers toward spreading the news of the coming of the New Jerusalem.

You Are Needed:

"We must encourage, cheer, uplift and teach all who will listen to the call of the Christ that they may be gathered into the New Jerusalem. There is no place for drones. For once we have vowed allegiance to the Christ and His work; the great Law of the Universe will force ns to fulfil our vows or pay the penalty. Thus we must become either helpers and redeemers of mankind or stumbling blocks in its path. If we refuse to take a firm stand on the positive side of good, we are swept into the negative current.

The New Jerusalem:

"The New Jerusalem has existed throughout eternity as a perfect and ideal state of humanity, but it has only existed in the higher realms, and only in our Higher Selves have we been able to dwell in its mansions. If it is to become a reality upon the physical plane its manifestation must be accomplished by the united efforts of all sincere and devoted followers of the Christ who are awakened to this possibility. We must begin with ourselves. The New Jerusalem can manifest within us, but we must permit the King of Righteousness not only to enter into His tabernacle, but *dwell therein*. Our hearts and minds and bodies must literally be made holy temples, sanctuaries of the Most High.

Sacred Sanctuaries:

"The first step then in this great coming of the Lord is to prepare our tabernacles. It is useless to look forward to the founding of an ideal dry or center of civilization in some favored spot on earth, where the Gods or the godpowers shall incarnate in a perfected manhood and womanhood, where the Great Ones shall teach mankind face to face and establish the reign of love and justice, unless we begin the preparation for such manifestations in our own hearts and minds and lives. For unless we can build within ourselves sacred sanctuaries in which the godpowers can dwell and manifest and enable us to live in love and fellowship with our brothers and sisters, how can we expect to associate with the Great Ones?"

From *The New Jerusalem* (Released April 7, 1913).

Karma:

Extract from a letter to a student of the Order of Christian Mystics: "In reply to your question as to the Lords of

Karma, the winds and the Allies, we are directed to say that Karma always includes several kinds: personal, sectional (environmental), national, racial and world karma. It is like a cord made up of several strands, each strand being made up of innumerable threads.

World Karma:

World karma necessarily affects all humanity through the seasonal changes, through world disasters, wars, etc, sufficiently great to affect all. This general world karma is modified in different regions by each region's national karma, sectional climatic changes, storms, disasters, etc., and still further by the personal karma of its inhabitants.

National Karma:

Thus, national karma is a determining factor in the national spirit, national environment, national reactions, etc, and determines to what extent the nation shall participate in the world karma.

Personal Karma:

The personal karma gives the individual his place and determines his reaction to the national karma, namely, to what extent he personally shall participate in it; for instance, whether he will be drafted in such times as these, and where he will be assigned when drafted, whether at the front or somewhere in the rear.

The Four Winds:

The mystical winds referred to in our lesson on *The Four Winds* [1] are one of the currents of force used by the great Lords of Karma to bring about on earth the conditions which will make the working out of these various lines of karma possible, the physical winds being used as one agency or instrument to bring this to pass.

Persons Involved:

Thus, when a great catastrophe occurs such as an earthquake, the holocaust at Halifax, the failure of crops, etc., it is the result, first, of world karma, inasmuch as the world currents there find a focal point for expression, yet all the other lines of karma must also operate in and through it, thus modifying it. No one whose personal karma did not call for such an experience would be present at those points at the time, or if present would have what might

---

[1] See chapter "The Four Winds" in *The Message of Aquaria*, Curtiss, 128.

seem to be a miraculous escape such as are recorded in every great catastrophe.

Good from Evil:

Yet the karma of even those who passed through the catastrophe may not have been preponderatingly bad, for in many cases only such a crushing blow could stir their hearts and awaken them out of their selfishness and call forth and develop their human sympathy and compassion for others, which up to that time may have been dormant or at least unexpressed. If one could see such disasters from the higher planes he would see many more bright and golden threads than black ones.

The North Wind:

As to the storms and winds fighting against the interests of the Allies through disturbance to their shipping, depots, movement of troops, etc, again we have to consider world, national and regional karma. The mystical North Wind is the one given power in these last days to sweep away old conditions and make ready for the new, just as the physical North wind does with the vegetation of the past season. If national and regional karma brings the

Allies into its path in a region where it is fulfilling its appointed work, the most that can be done is to modify its intensity in accordance with the good karma present in the national, environmental and' personal karma of those in its path, where under normal conditions they were not supposed to be. It is much as though a mouse ran out of its hole directly in front of the broom with which the housemaid was cleaning the room, although she had no intention of hurting the mouse or even disturbing it.

Meager Reports:

It is scarcely possible for the mind of the average man untrained in the metaphysics of the manifestation of the Great Law to understand why the Germans, who are giving expression to its destructive aspect, seem not to suffer from like disasters of nature or do not have to contend against them to the same extent. The most obvious reason is that full reports of the disasters from which they suffer do not reach our ears.

Chastening:

But as to the occultism of it, if you take a broader and higher and wider view and realize the inner meaning of the text, "Whom the Lord loveth He chasteneth, and scourgeth every son whom he receiveth. If ye endure chastening God dealeth with you as sons;.... but if ye be without chastisement,.... then ye are bastards and not sons," you will begin to understand the reasons.

The Ally's Test:

In other words, the Allies as nations have reached a point where they are ready to pass the great and final test of the chastisement of sonship which, for all who "can endure to the end/' will mark a new day in the manifestation of universal brotherhood.

Injustice:

He who tolerates injustice is creating injustice within himself. And the more longsuffering either a nation or an individual is under injustice, the more they dwell upon and create it. Hence when the revolt, or time of expression comes, they will express the very injustices and cruelties upon which they have so long brooded."

CHAPTER V

PERMANENT PEACE, GOD'S PLAN[1]

> "And he shall judge among many people, and rebuke strong nations afar; and they shall beat their swords into plowshares, and their spears into pruning hooks; nation shall not lift up sword against nation, neither shall they learn war any more,"
> *Micah*, iv, 3-4.

God's Plan:

All things come into outer manifestation from that which is within.[2] To achieve Permanent Peace in the world we must teach the nations of the world that Permanent Peace is God's plan for the world and man's ultimate destiny, hence it is bound to come. But since man has free-will to follow his own desires it is possible to bring about peace quickly or to push it back and go on for ages suffering the misery of periodic wars.

---

[1] Released July 7th, 1915.
[2] For details see *Why Are We Here?* Curtiss.

See the Vision:

To begin in earnest to work for Permanent Peace we must first believe in and reach up to the beatific vision so graphically described by the prophets Isaiah and Micah, then begin within our own hearts and lives to manifest it. For only as we bring our minds and lives into harmony with God's plan can we manifest mental and bodily harmony here on earth. *And there can be no peace and harmony among nations except as an expression of peace and harmony within the individuals of the nations.*

The Divine Plan:

Therefore the individual Permanent Peace means first, the recognition of the Divine Plan; a realization that nineteen hundred years ago when the heavens opened and in the darkness of humanity's mental night the angels appeared to the simple shepherds and declared: "Peace on earth, good will toward man," it was not a mere travesty, a Utopian dream never to be materialized. It was the announcement of one more important step toward the fulfilment of the same Divine Plan announced by the prophets of old, and which through all the ages has slowly but surely been descending and taking form on earth, because it already existed in heaven.

Man's Mistake:

The mistake mankind has made is in thinking that the angels were proclaiming its full and perfect accomplishment at that time, when even yet it has not come to pass. This is because the race is still manifesting [1] in its fifth day-period, and we are told that man must labor through six full days,[1] and that only on the seventh day can he rest in the ultimate fulfilment.

Periods Needed:

Just as it required six long periods to create the physical earth on which man's physical expression could dwell and manifest to perfection, so must it take six periods or "days of labor" to create man's mental and spiritual dwelling place in which to unfold and fulfil his mental and spiritual destiny. For this Permanent Peace is a prime necessity. Without it he cannot find his rest on the seventh day or survey his creations and say that they are good.

---

[1] For details see *The Key to the Universe*, Curtiss, 201.

War a Shock:

If this world war today is a shock to our ideals of peace, harmony and righteousness, think of the shock to the faith of the shepherds when Herod made his bloody war upon the innocent babes so soon after the announcement of the angelic hosts; also when Jesus himself, whom they expected to bring peace and good will to all the world and restore the kingdom of Israel, was led away to be crucified and His followers, scattered, not one among them standing by Him to the end!

Hearts Must Respond:

Yet in spite of all these seeming contradictions and the long delay in the coming of the promised peace, the angels' song was not a mistake. Peace had already been born in the heaven world, hence must inevitably descend to earth in the fulness of time, for it is God's plan for this world. It will descend into manifestation on earth just *as soon as the hearts of humanity respond* to it and give it lodgment in sufficient numbers to express it, even though humanity has been struggling toward it for nineteen hundred years with seemingly little progress.

The Angels' Song:

Just as the birth of the Christ must take place in each heart ere the fulness of the Christ can reign on earth, so must the angels' song which announced that birth, be sung in every heart. Every Soul must respond and prepare the conditions in his or her own heart and life ere we can hope for Permanent Peace among the nations of the earth.

Banish Ignorance:

Only as we deal with the world, just as we deal with our own lives, can we attain Permanent Peace. As long as darkness, ignorance and superstition reign in the minds of a majority of mankind, the mind of the world cannot be at peace.

Power of Thought:

Yet such is the creative power of thought that many minds at peace and thinking peace for all mankind, including their own personal enemies, will spread the thought to the minds of others and make it contagious so that ere we know it war will be done with forever. Only then will we see the swords of the nations turned into plowshares, and peaceful pursuits taking the place of war. But as long as a majority of mankind believe that wealth, commerce, power and worldly position are the things to be striven for above all else, there can be no Permanent Peace.

Role of Wealth and Power:

While wealth, commerce, power, etc, are inevitable and necessary for a nation's prosperity, they should be the *results or by-products* of the nation's attainments, rather than the ideals for which it strives. Hence while a nation holds for its ideals such sentiments as, "Let him take who has the power. Let him hold who can," or "To the victor belongs the spoils," etc., and forgets that the angels' song can never be fulfilled until a majority of mankind obeys the first part of that song, namely, "Glory to God in the highest," peace on earth and the good will toward mankind, peace cannot be permanent.

Cease Resistance:

For the underlying mysticism of true peace is oneness of purpose with the Divine Plan, the *ceasing of the resistance of man to the guidance of the Divine*; a realization that that which is created by man's desire and fructified by his power of thought is the thing which will inevitably manifest in the outer life, both of the individual and the race.

The Father's Will:

From the very dawn of creation when God said: "Let there be light" and there was light, the great war of the darkness against responding to the Light; of matter resisting Spirit; man resisting the call of the Divine, has been going on. And all war on the physical plane is but the outer manifestation of this mystical inner warfare which is forever being' waged in the invisible side of life. And it will continue to be waged until man learns to do the will of the Father-in-heaven, on earth, with as little friction and resistance as it is done in heaven.

Recognize Conditions:

Like all malignant diseases, that which is in the blood or in the life-stream must come forth into expression in the body ere it can be recognized, healed and fully eradicated. And when it breaks out or comes to a definite head it has already taken the first step toward its cure and eradication from the system.

The World Disease:

The world today has broken out with a most malignant disease, *i.e.*, extreme nationalism (national selfishness), pride and lust for power and supremacy. This disease has been in the blood of humanity in a chronic form for ages, and although it has broken out periodically again and again in various wars and in the horrors of "man's inhumanity to man," yet it has never been eradicated from the system, because heretofore mankind has never attacked *its cause*, but has dealt merely with its symptoms.

Seek for the Cure:

The present war, however, has broken out with such terrible malignity that it has aroused the world as never before to the necessity for *a permanent cure*, no matter what the cost. May we never cease to seek for the cure until it is found!

World Suffering:

Hence in every nation and country we find serious efforts being made to diagnose the disease, to seek out its hidden causes and apply the remedy. No more temporizing with symptoms will suffice. *It must be a radical cure.* For the world today is realizing as never before, the universal brotherhood of races, hence that, like parts of the human body, no one nation can be desolated by war and suffer without the whole human family's suffering with it

Operation Needed:

Even those who live in a neutral country cannot hope wholly to escape it, for it is a festering ulcer on the body of humanity and must affect the whole organism. And since the men of the race are occupied in the surgical operation of removing the ulcer with their swords, it is high time that the women of the race not only support them in their efforts but take up the work of permanent cure, just as the women of Europe are nursing and bringing about the permanent cure of the individual bodies of the wounded.

Woman's Mission:

This then is woman's mission. *First*, to see the vision of the ideal to be attained and the reason for its failure to manifest in the past; and *second*, fearlessly and devotedly with no thought of the stupendousness of the task, to undertake to bring sanity to the mind and health to the body of humanity as a whole.

Michael vs. the Dragon:

The *Bible* tells us that there was war in heaven. "Michael and his angels fought against the dragon; and the dragon fought and his angels, and prevailed not; neither was their place found any more in heaven." This has been confused in the minds of many with the descent of Lucifer (meaning "the shining one") the Light Bearer, because of the passages, "I beheld Satan as lightning fall from heaven," and "How are thou fallen from heaven, O Lucifer, son of the morning!" but the meanings of the two allegories are quite different.

War in Heaven:

The war in heaven, as we have already said, was the war between Spirit and matter in the higher realms, the word heaven being used here to indicate the realms of the higher astral world. Michael is the Angel of the Sun from which proceeds the true spiritual creative force which we call the Christ-principle.

Dragon's Symbol:

The dragon typifies the perverted and degraded creative force which man has relegated and confined to its expression through the physical creative centers, by whose perversion and degradation he has brought forth all the evil that manifests on earth today.

The Tester:

The Angel who fell from heaven, like the fearful and devastating force of lightning, is Saturn, the great Tester and Initiator. Lightning is the result of the bursting forth of the electrical potential stored up in a thunder-cloud and as we have said elsewhere[1] all storms are the result of man's inharmony. Hence lightning, like Saturn, is both the tester and readjuster or the bringer to earth of the stored-up inharmony resulting from man's disobedience and. resistance to the Divine Law.

The Adversary:

Yet Saturn is neither man's enemy nor the devil, as he is so often miscalled, but is the adversary in the sense of forcing man to a realization of his disobedience and precipitating the karmic results upon him. Yet, like lightning, tills precipitation is the only way to dissipate the old Karma and purify the atmosphere of the Soul.

---

[1] See *The Voice of Isis*, Curtiss, 116.

Lucifer:

On the other hand, Lucifer, Son of the Morning, is the symbol of the necessary descent of the Christ-principle to earth that it may clothe itself in matter and by its manifestation in that dense expression uplift, spiritualize and redeem matter.

Two Allegories:

In these two allegories we have not only the explanation of the war in heaven, but of every war that has ever raged on earth or within the heart of man, whether of actual slaughter and bloodshed, mental struggle and warfare or any other form of man's inharmony which wars against God's perfect Plan of Creation, *i.e.*, Perfect Peace.

The Pacifists:

For remember that God's plan is Permanent Peace, but not the "peace at any price" of the pacifists, for we see that the Divine Law is that there can be Permanent Peace only when all antagonism and inharmony has been transmuted into harmony. Until this has taken place we may cry "Peace I Peace I" eternally, but there can be no peace.

Saturn's Fall:

Therefore while Saturn "fell" to earth in seeming rebellion, in reality he was the Light Bearer, the lightning which pierced the contented darkness of earth conditions and made the expression of the Light in that darkness. Think of it! an Archangel from heaven giving up the bliss and happiness of his spiritual estate that he might dispel the clouds of ignorance and bring to mankind the spiritual Light! just as a lightning stroke breaks up the storm clouds surcharged with electrical energy and brings to earth the purifying and energizing ozone of the upper strata of the air.

The Angel of Peace:

The mighty struggle in Europe today seems to many of you but another Angel fallen from your heaven world, namely the Angel of Civilization and of your higher ideals and Christprinciples. Yet back of this fall, as of the first Angel, those of you who are patiently watching on the heights of the mountainside, keeping guard over the flocks of your thoughts and desires through this dark night, and who are straining your mental eyes into the black darkness of carnage, you will see that the Angel is in reality the Angel of Permanent Peace.

Civilization Requires Harmony:

You will see that *civilisation could never permanently endure* until this Angel of Peace had penetrated into the clouds of inharmony and unbrotherliness which hung over humanity and shut out the Light of the Spiritual Sun, and like a lightning stroke precipitated them as this great cloudburst of war. Only thus could the blackest night the world has ever seen respond to the same clarion cry, "Glory to God in the highest, ye sons of men. For only thus can there be peace on earth and good will toward men."

Woman's Initiative:

Is man too busy with war to listen? Must he go on blindly killing and being killed? Then it is woman who must be the watcher on the mountain side to proclaim the vision. It must be the true womanhood of the race which must open a path through the dense atmosphere of carnage, that through it the Angel hosts can enter.

Insist on Manifestation:

It must be true womanhood who through the din of battle must listen for the Song of Permanent Peace, and hearing it, with the faith and courage of her womanhood, prepare for and insist upon its manifestation.

The Bringer-forth:

Only woman is equal to the occasion, for woman's great gift is the power to bring forth. And only through the power of enlightened womanhood can the seeds being sown in this terrible night of war bring forth the fruits of Permanent Peace to the world, which is destined to follow the dark night of war.

Inculcate Peace:

To accomplish this the women of the world should unite. There is work for all. Not only those who can speak for peace, but every mother can radiate and *inculcate peace* and the *peace ideal in the home*, no matter to what country she may give her allegiance.

Effect on Children:

At this time when the mental atmosphere of the world is infected with antagonism and hatred, there is a tendency to let trifles disturb us, and we find it harder than usual to control our tempers. And since the sensitive nature of the child is quick to respond to the currents of thought-force surrounding it, there is an increased tendency toward quarrelsomeness. The scientists tell us that even the ants, instead of making war for food or nest as formerly, now make war wantonly for the lust of fighting. Therefore each person should be especially watchful to *maintain peace within himself* and in the household during these trying days.

Ways of Helping:

There are many ways of helping to bring about Permanent Peace, and the promise of the Angels' song can be fulfilled every day, and the women can hasten its fulfilment in the world, by determining to live at peace within and with their neighbors, and doing some definite work for the spread of the idea of Permanent Peace.

The Babe Within:

The Babe whose birth was announced to mankind by the angelic chorus still lives in the sanctuary of each heart. But let us as a race determinedly unwind the swaddling clothes that hide Him from our sight and no longer keep Him in the manger where the animal desires go to feed! Let us proclaim Him at the right hand of God to whom we give "Glory in the highest!" Only so can the prophecy be wholly fulfilled in humanity.

Man's Destiny:

Therefore our work for Permanent Peace on earth must be carried on along the lines of God's Plan. We do not have to think out a plan of our own or seek for something new which we fear may be so Utopian that it cannot be accomplished. Instead we must take courage and be supremely confident, for *Permanent Peace is the destiny of mankind and cannot fail ultimately to materialize.* Yet since man is God's vice-regent on earth he can do much to hasten the day of the ultimate Permanent Peace, just as in the ages past he has done much to retard its manifestation.

The Heavens Open:

Even as we stand appalled at the devastation and ruin of this storm of war, let us lift our thoughts to God, see the heavens open and glimpse the Divine Plan. Though we be sore afraid, we will behold a multitude of the heavenly host and hear amidst the thunders of war the angelic voices singing; "Glory to God in the highest, and on earth peace and good will toward man."

A New Day Coming:

Thus will we realize that this terrible war is but another step toward the fulfilment of a new day for humanity, the great sixth day, and that on the morrow we shall abide forever in God's Permanent Peace.

CHAPTER VI

"THE WAR" OR THE PRINCIPLE OF RESISTANCE

> "It is only by the attractive force of the contrasts that the two opposites—Spirit and Matter—can be cemented together on Earth, and, smelted in the fire of self-conscious experience and suffering, find themselves wedded in Eternity. This will reveal the meaning of many hitherto incomprehensible allegories, foolishly called 'fables.'"
> *The Secret Doctrine*, Blavatsky, vol. ii, 108.

As Above, So Below:

It is an axiom in our Cosmic Soul Science that there can be no manifestation without duality, no shadow without its Reality. According to our cosmic philosophy everything that manifests descends from above, its expression on earth being but the shadow or reflection of a Reality in the higher realms. "St Paul.... called our World, 'the enigmatical mirror of pure truth/ and St. Gregory of Nazianzen corroborated Hermes by stating that: 'Things visible are but the shadow and delineation of things that we cannot see.'. . . . 'All that is on earth, saith the Lord (Ormazd), *is the shadow of something that is in the superior spheres.*'. . . . It is an eternal combination, and images are repeated from the higher rung of the Ladder of Being down to the lower. . . . the lower 'mirror' disfiguring the image of the superior 'mirror.'"[1]

War a Shadow:

The *Zohar* also holds strongly to the idea that everything manifested in the Universe is the shadow of the Eternal Light or Deity, separated by the prism of Matter into its seven rays, each with its dual principle of light and shadow. Of what, then, is war on earth the shadow?

Equilibrium Disturbed:

In the beginning of the universe, the first emanation from the Absolute coming into manifestation necessarily had its positive and negative aspects or poles, Spirit and Substance. From the very dawn of the going forth of the Manifested from out the bosom of the Unmanifested, the state of perfect equilibrium was disturbed and the mighty *urge toward union* and

---

[1] *The Secret Doctrine*, Blavatsky, vol, ii. 280.

a restoration of the primordial equilibrium came into manifestation.

Cause of "The War:"

It is this *urge toward the restoration of the Projected to its Source*; the call of the Spirit to Matter; the Father to the Son; the Heavenly Man to the human; the Higher Self to the lower personality; that is the cause back of all war, all desire, hence back of all evolution. For *only in a union with its Cause* can the Cycle of Necessity be ended, the desire be satisfied and become one with the Will of the Father, "the War" ended, and the evolution be completed.

Principle of Resistance:

But the impelling Force which caused the outgoing or downward arc of projection into Manifestation naturally *resists the Indrawing power* or upward arc of Realization which is necessary to complete the At-one-ment. This *resistance* to the uplifting, dematerializing and indrawing force constitutes and is the basic principle back of all reflections, frictions, conflicts or phases of *"the War."*

Spirit Descends:

In the physical world this resistance is expressed as the war between Spirit and Matter; the resistance due to the density and inertia of Matter to the unfoldment and expression of the Spirit With the descent of the Light, Spirit clothed itself in Matter, not only that it might have expression but that it might evolve up through matter and by so doing spiritualize it and return it to its primordial state.

Lack of Response:

It is the inability of the lower vibrations of Matter to respond to the higher vibrations of Spirit that causes the resistance *until*, through the subliming and etherializing process which results from the friction thus engendered, Matter becomes finer and more plastic and thus more responsive to the expressions of Spirit.

Overcoming Resistance:

Hence in all cosmogonies, "'There were many Wars/ all referring to the struggles of adjustment, spiritual, cosmical and astronomical, but chiefly to the mysteries of the evolution of man, as he is now."[1] The point we wish to

---

[1] *The Secret Doctrine*, Blavatsky, i, 215.

"The War" or the Principle of Resistance 79

emphasize is that these types of "the war" are all *necessary factors* in the *overcoming of resistance* and in the adjustment which *must occur* ere the close of any and every major cycle.

Cosmic War:

There are accounts of three distinct Wars to be traced in almost every cosmogony. The first War happened in the night of time, between the Gods and the (A)-suras, and lasted for a period of one Divine Year."[1] Thus *"the War"* began with the "War in Heaven" or the resistance of certain expressions of the Godhead to carrying out the Divine Will; again, the *resistance* of the lower to the higher Will. This is far more than merely an expression of the Sun-Myth or the personification of the forces of nature, the war between Light and Darkness:

The Sun Myth:

For the various versions of the Sun-Myth[2] are but allegories expressing the cosmic principle of the *resistance of Matter* to the expression of Spirit, whether it be represented by the Christian Michael, the Angel of the Sun, slay-

---

[1] Ibid., i, 451. A Divine Year is 360 times a Day of Brahm (4320,000,000 years).
[2] See lesson *The Universal Solar Myth*, Curtiss.

ing the Apocalyptic Dragon; Horus, the Egyptian Sun-god, slaying Typhon, the Dragon Apophis; Hercules strangling the Python in his cradle, or Phoibos-Apollo, the Greek Helios, the Sun, 'the Light and Life of the World'.... who at the moment of his birth asks for his bow to kill Python, the Demon Dragon.[1]

The Eternal Struggle:

They all symbolize *the eternal struggle for light, progress and evolution* which constitutes the war between the Light of Wisdom and the Darkness of Ignorance; between unselfishness and selfishness; between the good of the whole and the ambitions of the few; between civilization and barbarism; between the Angel of Peace and the Dragon of Material Force embodied in Militarism; between Right and Might, etc.

Struggles for Control:

The second great phase of "*the War*" as reflected in humanity, occurred after the creation of man, when the *resistance* set up by the desires of the lower animal man to the Will of the Higher was exemplified in the struggle which took place between the Lunar and Solar Fathers.

---

[1] *The Secret Doctrine*, Blavatsky, ii, 400.

Creation of Man:

Cosmic philosophy teaches that the physical body or animal man was projected as a "shadow" or was "created" by the Hierarchy of the Lunar Fathers.[1] But the "man" so created was but a human animal without intellect or the spark of self-consciousness; he had not yet become "a living soul." As soon as the human animal had been perfected, the Hierarchy of the Solar Fathers—called "Sons of Mind"—projected into that animal form a "Ray" of themselves which became the Divine Spark, the individual, immortal Spiritual Ego, or, as the *Bible* puts it, they: "Breathed into his nostrils the Breath of Life (breath always being a symbol of Spirit); and (only then) man became a living (immortal) Soul."[2]

Physical Man a Product:

Man was thus the product of two distinct lines of creative forces, a semiterrestrial and a Divine; just as a mother brings forth (creates) the terrestrial body of her child, yet has nothing to do with making it "a living Soul."

---

[1] For *The Origin of Man*, see Chapter XVII, in *The Voice of Isis*, Curtiss.
[2] *Genesis*, ii. 7.

The Second Phase:

With the incarnating of the Spirit and the lighting of the spark of self-consciousness in man this second phase of "*the War*" began, *i.e.*, the effort of the spiritual Solar Fathers, through the incarnated Ray of Spirit or the Real Man, to control and guide the animal man, to the end that he might willingly respond to the higher law or Divine Will.

Instinct vs. Free-will:

The control of the Lunar Fathers had been through *instinct* and did not admit of the power of choice, while the control of the Solar Fathers was and is attained through the *free-will choice* of man, even though through his refusal to choose the higher guidance *he creates the suffering* by which he learns the unwisdom of that choice. The struggle was brought about, therefore, by the *resistance* offered by the animal instincts and the desires of the senses to voluntarily submitting to the uplifting and spiritualizing control of the Divine Will of the Real Man or Father-in-heaven.

Resistance of Intellect:

In the mental world "*the War*" manifests as the *resistance* of the Intellect to the promptings of Intuition; the temporary refusal of the Head to obey the promptings of the Heart. Until the self-conscious stage of man was reached the resistance was more or less passive or the resistance of inertia, but with the dawn of freewill and the power of choice the resistance became active and the animal element of antagonism was added to the inertia.

St. Paul's Recognition:

The light of self-consciousness and the development of the Intellect were the direct result of the incarnating Spirit's gradually evolving an adequate instrument by means of which it could relate itself in consciousness to the conditions of material manifestation. Then it could express itself in such conditions, as soon as the spark of Divine Mind burst into the flame of self-consciousness. The human animal thus awakened to itself—but as yet unable to recognize its Divine Parent—placed Intellect upon the throne as the source of its highest guidance.

Self-consciousness:

St Paul refers to this phase of "*the War*" when he says: "When I would do good (*i.e.*, follow the Intuitions from the Higher Self), behold evil (or the desires of the lower man) is present with me." It is *"the War"* manifesting between Higher and Lower Manas or the *resistance* of the human or intellectual consciousness to the Illumination and guidance of the Divine.

A Willing Servant:

And this phase of *"the War"* will continue in man until, by the subliming and spiritualizing process due to the friction (suffering) engendered, the Intellect will admit that it is but the creature and instrument; until it becomes the willing servant of the Real Man or Higher Self, and translates the Inspiration of the Spirit into terms of human consciousness which shall enable the human personality consciously to follow the Divine Guidance.

Man, the Arbitrator:

Of all creatures man alone has within him both the Higher Mind—the embodied Ray from the Divine Mind—and also the Lower Mind which is synthetized by the animal soul and has its highest expression through Intellect. Hence man is the Arbitrator, for he can reach up and comprehend God and also reach down into the animal consciousness and comprehend the resistance of matter and the views and arguments of the Lower Mind.

Man's Curses:

By the creative power of his thought he leaves the impress of his stage of evolution upon all the lower kingdoms. For just as *"the War"* in heaven was reflected in man, so has man reflected upon the lower kingdoms *"the War"* that is going on within himself. So it is through man, who has stamped the impress of his imperfections—the incomplete stage of his spiritual unfoldment—upon animal, vegetable and mineral as antagonism, hatred, disease and death, that the curse has been fulfilled: "Cursed is the ground for thy sake. . . . thorns also and thistles shall it bring forth to thee. . . . in the sweat of thy face shalt thou eat bread, till thou return unto the ground (his Source); for out of it wast thou taken; for dust thou art and unto dust shalt thou return."[1]

Dust of the Ground:

Looking at *"the War"* as symbolized by this so-called curse, with the eye of Spirit, we see

---

[1] *Genesis.* ii, 7.

that this curse contains a prophecy of the end of *"the War" i.e.*, the ultimate victory of the Spiritual over the mere animal man. Only that which is made of cosmic dust or Matter can be cursed by man's disobedience to the Divine Will. In other words, only that which man received from his Lunar ancestors—his physical, astral and desire bodies—can be said to be made of "dust" or the unredeemed matter of former world-periods[1] which formed the chaos into which the spiritual Light descended at the beginning of this cosmic Day of Evolution.

Transmutation:

Hence the so-called curse may be turned into a blessing, since it assures us that ultimately all that is dust (matter) will be returned to its Source at the end of *"the War"* but with the results of man's higher spiritual understanding of the great mystery of transmutation or redemption impressed upon it. The curse also tells us in a few cryptic words that the cause of *"the War"* is the effort of Spirit to redeem (literally "buy back" or return to its Source) Matter.

---

[1] See *The Voice of Isis*, Curtiss, Chapter XXIV.

Plan of Redemption:

Perhaps the position of man in this great struggle can be better comprehended if we consider an earthly simile. In an earthly war only one who has had experience on both sides or who is so gifted that he can enter fully and understandingly into the point of view of both combatants, is fitted to become an Arbitrator. In the mighty war between Spirit and Matter, man is such an Arbitrator; for he can, if he will, reach up into the Spiritual Consciousness and comprehend the Divine Plan of Redemption, the power of the Spiritual Consciousness to uplift the animal consciousness; can grasp the reality of the transmuting power of Divine Love, and understand that only through the reign of the Heart can there be peace; for the Intellect, when its dominance is insisted upon, can but prolong "*the War*".

Intellect and Intuition:

He can also make his Intellect a powerful servant which can descend into the most microscopic details of Matter and understand the point of view and the cause for which the lower man fights. Through the Light of Intuition he can ascend into the higher realms and grasp the macrocosmic details of the Grand Plan and realize that through Intellect alone he can never correlate with the Spirit of that which the Intellect has discovered.

The Curse Removed:

Thus from his position as Arbitrator he can look down not only into the suffering, misery and crime created by the resistance of the selfish animal desires, but can also see how *only through the spirit* of Love and Harmony and through Obedience to the guidance of the Spirit can man and nature be redeemed and the curse be removed.

Victories of Mind:

The victories of the lower mind are precipitated in its home-world—the physical consciousness—as mental and emotional storms, while the victories of the Higher Mind are accumulated in its home-world as so much added power of the Spirit to manifest on earth both for the individual, the Race and the planet.

Legends:

"*The War*" between the Higher and Lower Selves therefore began when the child of the

Lunar Fathers became also the child of the Solar Fathers. Hence we find throughout all myth and allegory the frequent reference to wars between the Sun-gods and the Moon-gods or between the Priests of the Sun and the Priests of the Moon. And in the early races, the Sun-gods "walked and talked with men," that is, through their Divine Incarnations as great Spiritual Teachers, the Sun-gods taught the intellectually-infant humanity the principles of all arts, sciences and philosophies. Many of these are today temporarily lost because of the present wave of materialism.

The Masses Unresponsive:

The great mass of the Race was unable to respond to that higher guidance except for a short time, and there arose a division into two groups, the smaller of which still followed the Divine Teachers, and the larger which followed the call of sense gratification and selfishness represented by the Priests of the Moon-god. As Éliphas Lévi says: "Men grew weary of the light, took refuge in the shadow of bodily substance; the dream of the void, which is filled by God, soon appeared to be greater than God himself in their eyes and thus Hell was created."

The Third Phase:

The third great phase of "*the War*" therefore manifested on earth in the terrible struggle which took place at the close of the Fourth or Atlantean Race between Rama, the first of the Divine Dynasty or Solar Kings of the early Aryan Race, and Ravana, the leader of the scorcery-working Atlanteans.

Cause of Evolution:

As *The Secret Doctrine* tells us:[1] "With the Fifth, our own Race, the Lunar-solar worship divided the nations into distinct, antagonistic camps. It led to the events described eons later in the Mahabharatan War."[2] Whether we take this in its historical aspect or as a legendary reference to the escape of the Aryans from Atlantis; as Moses leading the Children of Israel out of Egypt; as the escape of the higher faculties from the bondage of the senses; or purely as an allegorical expression of the Sun-

---
[1] *The Secret Doctrine*, Blavatsky, i, 426.
[2] This served as a prototype. . . . for the Western nations to build their War of the Titans upon. . . . The War of the Titans is but a legendary and deified copy of the real war that took place. . . . It is the record of the terrible strife between the 'Sons of God' and the 'sons of Shadow' of the Fourth and Fifth Races. It is on these two events. . . . that every subsequent national tradition on the subject has been built."
The Secret Doctrine, Blavatsky, ii, 521

Myth, in each instance we have a leader who represents the Divine Dynasty or Light, Progress and Evolution—the *upward and indrawing* power which is the cause of all evolution, civilization, progress—and who always leads his followers in triumph over the hosts of opposition, which are inevitably swallowed up in the sea.

Divine Guidance:

In the *Bible* account this leader is called Moses, the Law-giver, while in the individual those faculties which *choose to follow* the Divine Law become the "chosen people." By following the Divine Guidance they are led out of the bondage of the senses and escape from the power of King Desire,[1] represented by Pharaoh. But King Desire is loath to let them escape him and pursues after them, only to be swallowed up in the waters of the Great Sea, even as the hosts of Ravana were swallowed up by the sinking of Atlantis.

War in the Body:

In the physical body "*the War*" is expressed through certain storms of bodily inharmony, illness or disaster which sweep over those who

---

[1] See chapter on *King Desire* in *The Inner Radiance*, Curtiss; also the lesson on *The Great Migration*, Curtiss.

are endeavoring to follow the Higher Guidance and striving to "live the life." When the ideal of a higher life is set up by the consciousness it sounds a new and higher key-note throughout the body. Those atoms which can respond, answer the call and follow the new Law-giver and are led out of bondage into the freedom of a new cycle or expression of Life. While in those atoms which belong wholly to the old dispensation, which have fulfilled their mission and are not sufficiently evolved to take on the higher vibration and enter the new cycle, the *resistance* to the higher call is so great that it brings on "*the War*" in which they are vanquished and sloughed out of the body through a cleansing cataclysm of illness. This, while it leaves the body temporarily devastated and weak, has nevertheless cleared the field of opposition and prepared for the manifestation of a higher expression of Life.

War in the Emotions:

In the mental world the outlet will be found through the emotions. The expression of these emotions becomes a storm which sweeps away the control of those who open the door of their minds through irritation, impatience, anger, jealousy, envy, animal desires, etc., and leaves them devastated, yet relieved and ready, in the next time of trial, for an encounter which shall be more successful in proportion to the effort made to conquer in the past.

Transmute Inharmony:

This, however, should not be made an excuse for giving way to emotional excitement of any kind for a strong effort should always be made for control and peace, *i.e.*, to *transmute inharmony* and turn its perverted forces into constructive and useful channels. But if a storm should gather and burst, be ready to set a higher standard and a greater degree of achievement in the period of reconstruction.

Initiation:

"The War" is also reflected in the terrible struggles through which the candidate for Mastery must pass during his Initiation; the struggle of the Christ within to slay the dragon of self; the Guardian Angel to slay the Dweller on the Threshold. It is also exemplified in the *resistance* of humanity to new or higher spiritual teachings; the misunderstanding, misrepresentation, condemnation, slander, persecution,

final crucifixion *but ultimate triumph*, through which every Lightbearer who comes to humanity has to pass.

Law of Adjustment:

From the principles outlined above it will be seen that the wars among nations which ultimately make for enlightenment, civilization, freedom, the independence of each nation and the general advance of mankind, are not evidences of the failure of civilization or the failure of the particular religion which prevails at the time. They are but skirmishes in *"the War"*; expressions of the cosmic *Law of Adjustment* called Karma, by which that which is created by mankind must be faced and redeemed; that which is sown must be reaped. There must be periodic manifestations of *"the War"* as long as Matter *resists Spirit*; as long as barbarism resists civilization; civilization resists the Brotherhood of Nations; industry resists coöperation; materialism resists altruism and idealism, in short, as long as any phase of manifestation resists the call to progress by a higher power.

The Golden Age:

But the conflicts should grow fewer and fewer and the periods of peace be more and

"The War" or the Principle of Resistance 95

more prolonged in each succeeding upward cycle, until the Golden Age of the Seventh Great Race of man[1] is reached; until we return again to the rule of the Divine Kings—the "Sons of God" as the *Bible* calls them—among men, not as parents ruling over children, as in the beginning, but as Elder Brothers or Senior Partners whose experience and wisdom we gladly accept and follow.

The Great Lesson:

The great lesson to be learned from *"the War"* is that it is a very real and personal issue with each awakened Soul who has responded to the call of the Divine and donned the armor of the Christ and become a Soldier of the Cross. Each Soul is judged at the close of each lifecycle by the sum total of how much it has overcome, how much of the lower self it has illumined by the higher spiritual consciousness.

Real Success:

And strange as it may seem to some, the real evolution in man is gauged by how successfully he has fulfilled his mission as Arbitrator between Spirit and matter, between the higher

---

[1] For details see *The Voice of Isis*, Curtiss, Chapter XV.

kingdoms and the lower, giving to each its rightful place, while he himself stands calm and unmoved in the midst of *"the War"* confidently knowing that back of all the turmoil, inharmony and strife are "the everlasting arms" of Divine Love, and that the true Peace is ever hovering, like the Breath of God, over the seeming chaos.[1]

---

[1] Written September 30, 1914.

CHAPTER VII

THE BATTLE OF ARMAGEDDON[1]

> "To whom shall I speak, and give warning, that they may hear? behold, their ear is uncircumcised, and they cannot harken: behold the word of the Lord is unto them a reproach; they have no delight in it."
> *Jeremiah*, vi, 10.

> "And I saw three unclean spirits like frogs come out of the mouth of the dragon, and out of the mouth of the beast, and out of the mouth of the false prophet. For they are the spirits of devils, working miracles, which go forth unto the kings of the whole earth and of the whole world, to gather them to the battle of that great day of God Almighty. . . . And he gathered them together into a place called in the Hebrew tongue Armageddon."
> *Revelation*, xvi, 13-16.

Meaning of Armageddon:

The literal meaning of Armageddon is "on the heights" or "on high," and in this sense it is used to designate the invisible realms of the astral plane. The hosts which are gathered to this great battle are the hosts of the accumulated thought-forms of lust, greed, envy, hate, selfishness and unbrotherliness engendered by

---

[1] Released in 1909. See *The Book of Enoch*, Chapter IX.

the wrong thinking of humanity from the beginning, as well as the *results* of their evil words and deeds, all of which are ever seeking expression through their creators.

Fruit of Thought:

Jeremiah specifically refers to these *forces as causes* when he says: "Hear, O earth: behold, I will bring evil upon this people, *even the fruit of their thoughts*, because they have not hearkened unto my words, nor my law, but rejected it."[1] During this battle all the stored-up evil must have a focus through which it can pour itself out upon the lowest or physical plane where its precipitation will end the cycle of its manifestation.

Time Is at Hand:

These forces have accumulated because, during the childhood of the Race the Masters of Wisdom and the Rulers of the sub-races have held the forces back until the Race grew strong enough to bear them upon its own shoulders; grew up, as it were. But the Race has now grown up. The cycle is closing and the time for the adjustment is at hand. "Therefore I

---

[1] *Jeremiah*, vi, 19.

am full of the fury of the Lord (Law); I am weary with holding in: I will pour it out upon the children abroad, and upon the assembly of young men together."[1]

Human Instruments:

And there is invariably found some human being who, because of his prominence and because of his habit of opening his mind to the insinuating flattery and fatuous promises of great attainments, or *perhaps world dominion,* from the astral leaders—whom the Bible refers to as "the rulers of the darkness of this world"—becomes the executor or mouthpiece of the stored-up evil forces or the channel through which they find expression in the physical world, as for instance, Nero, the Borgias, and others in later eras. In this way the evil and unredeemed Karma is adjusted so as to permit the good aspect of the forces involved to be extracted, just as ore is crushed or melted that the gold may be extracted.

Self-Chosen Ones:

Often such an one believes himself to be the chosen of the Lord, chosen to cleanse the world

---

[1] *Jeremiah,* vi. 11.

or to impose his idea of culture upon it; for the dominant Principalities of Evil have convinced him that they are the "Voice of God," and he prides himself on being their obedient servant.

Egotistical Leaders:

While many referred to the last European conflict as Armageddon, the meaning of the word shows that war is but one reflection or outpouring on earth of the real battle that has been raging in the higher realms. It is precipitated now because another earthly channel has been found in the person of a leader sufficiently egotistical, presumptuous and selfrighteous to listen to the flattery of the obsessing astral entities and become the earthly advocate of those powers of darkness.

War and Cataclysms:

The working out and adjustment of these karmic forces must take place at the close of each Race, and in a lesser degree at the close of each sub-race. This adjustment precipitates the great race wars which are followed by the cataclysms which mark the close of sub-races and Races; for every particle of matter composing the Race-continents, as well as every particle in the body of individual man, must have its own individual balancing, purification, readjustment and ultimate redemption, that it may be ready for the same people when they reincarnate again.

Sinking of Atlantis:

The last great racial Armageddon occurred just before the sinking of the continent of Atlantis, at the close of the cycle of the Fourth Great Race (Atlantean). "This hints at the struggle between the 'sons of God' and the Sons of the Dark Wisdom—our forefathers; or between the Atlanteans and the Aryan Adepts. The whole history of that period is allegorized in the *Ramayana* which is the mystic narrative in epic form of the struggle between Rama—the first king of the Divine Dynasty of the early Aryans and the agent of the white forces—and Ravana, the symbolic personification of the Atlantean (Lanka) Race and the agent of the Black forces. The former were the incarnations of the Solar Gods; the latter, of the Lunar Devas.

Battle of Good and Evil:

This was the great battle between Good and Evil, between White and Black Magic, for the supremacy of the divine forces over the lower terrestrial, or cosmic powers."[1] The sinking of the continent of Atlantis which followed was the balancing of the accounts of the entire Fourth Race. It was a necessary preparation (through the purifying action of the salt water) of the continent for a future Race.

The Survivors:

The survivors—those who were sufficiently spiritualized, awakened and obedient, to follow their Divine Rulers—were picked out, separated and trained by the Masters long before the sinking of the continent, and became the seed of the present Fifth (Aryan) Great Race, just as some are now being chosen and trained for a similar function.

Sub-race Karma:

Ere this present Fifth race ends—and we are now just entering upon its sixth sub-race[2]—a similar adjustment of its Race Karma must take place, and it has now already begun its physical manifestation. The great European war now raging offers a focal point through which the

---

[1] *The Secret Doctrine*, Blavatsky, ii, 520.
[2] See *The Voice of Isis*, Curtiss, Chapter XVII.

Karma of the fifth sub-race of the Aryans can be precipitated on the physical plane and adjusted.

A Deluded Leader:

For it is the beginning of the great period which will mark the close of the Fifth Great Race. And in Emperor William of Germany[1] a leader has been found who could be so deluded and obsessed as to be used as the tool of the dark forces. But we must remember the words of Jesus: "It must needs be that offences come; but woe to that man by whom the offence cometh." Therefore, while we must condemn his acts we must also pity and pray for the man.

Europe, the Focal Point:

Europe is the first focal point because it was in Europe that the greater part of that Karma was engendered, *i.e.*, through the many bitter political wars which drenched its soil in blood; through the sectarian wars carried on in the name of the Church, but which perverted religion and made priest-craft a curse; and through the intolerance, selfishness, and mental and spiritual blindness of the religious leaders

---

[1] And now in Adolph Hitler.

which manifested in the mental war which finally culminated in the most inhuman persecutions the civilized world has ever known—the Inquisition.

The Inquisition:

Today we are reaping especially the Karma sown by the unspeakable cruelties practised by the Inquisition; for it stands as the great crime of the fifth sub-race. While it is true that Christians were burned and tortured in the earlier centuries by Nero and others, even what are called the pre-Christian atrocities were but the spawn out of which the Inquisition was hatched, and from that can be traced almost all the degrading crimes of the later days, especially intolerance and hatred and their results.

Inquisition in Germany:

We are apt to associate the Inquisition with Spain, yet Spain and her Western colonies did not institute the Inquisition until the year 1232, while in Italy, France, England and Germany it was in full swing, with intervals of cessation, from early in the sixth century. Especially in Germany, with Conrad of Marburg (called the "Terrible") as chief inquisitor, the cruelty was prosecuted with such extreme zeal as even to exceed the wishes of the Pope. The Inquisition was also established on the high seas in all galleys and ships. There the cruelties and punishments were beyond belief.

Astral Battles:

The battles of the physical world are fought on the physical plane with physical weapons, but the true battle of Armageddon must be fought first upon the astral plane with thoughts and psychic forces for weapons, the conflict now raging being but a pouring out of the evil and a gathering together of the forces of Good for the final battle on the higher planes.

Time of Adjustment:

This battle has already begun. And during the entire sixth sub-race of the present Fifth Great Race we may expect a more or less unsettled condition. For this is the time of adjustment; the time of struggle to overcome the evils which the Race as a whole has outlived, yet which it has not fully conquered and redeemed.

The Christ-force:

The number 6 is both the number of the Christ[1] and also of unrest. It symbolizes the

---

[1] See *The Key to the Universe*, Curtiss, 195.

mighty struggle of the Christ-force to penetrate into and transmute the evil and manifest itself. Hence only as humanity enters into the seventh sub-race will it have true and lasting world peace and rest; for God blessed the seventh day and hallowed it (also the seventh Race and each seventh sub-race is especially blessed), and during that period rested from His labors.

Coming Disasters:

Therefore the progress of the sixth sub-race into which we are now entering will be marked by tremendous disasters precipitated upon the physical plane[1] — wars, *unusual* earthquakes, cyclones, volcanic eruptions and meteoric showers, floods, etc. — of more or less severity until the final battle and cataclysm in which the battlefield and the defeated army will be swallowed up and a new and purified land shall rise out of the waters, during the sixth sub-race, for the new Sixth Great Race to inhabit. The victors will remain as the seed of the New Race to people the new land.

The First Battle:

The "final battle" does not refer to the end of this present war of nations, but to the close

---

[1] First published in 1909.

of the true battle of Armageddon of which *the present World War is but the first phase*.

Lemuria Rising:

The cataclysmic changes in the earth's surface will result in there rising out of the waters of the Pacific ocean the ancient Lemurian continent, which, during the entire seventh subrace, will pass through the various steps[1] necessary to make it a fit dwelling place for the Sixth Great Race.

The New Humanity:

Just as these changes must take place for the planet, so must they take place in humanity through bloody wars, strikes and other conflicts which will continue until all conflicts of man with man, and *man's resistance* to the Divine are swallowed up, and out of the waters of affliction there shall arise a new and greater humanity with true Brotherhood, Love, Peace, Harmony and Coöperation, as its watchword.

The time has now come when the accumulated mass of old Race Karma must be definitely met and conquered ere humanity can enter upon the new sub-race, its next step in evolution.

---

[1] See *The Voice of Isis*, Curtiss, 388.

The Dweller:

This, in a measure, is to the world what the Dweller on the Threshold is to the neophyte. And as with the neophyte before each important step is taken, it must be met and conquered. For just as the neophyte, through his evil thoughts, words and acts, has created an entitized form of evil—his individual Dweller—so the planet has been pouring out its evils throughout its long cycle until they have become entitized as a "dark planet" with a living Ruler, the Anti-Christ who definitely works through those who give themselves up to his guidance or obsession. This planet may be called the Dweller on the Threshold for humanity as a whole.

The Destroyer Planet:

The astronomers of Harvard University have already discovered the influence of this dark planet[1]—the Destroyer—which, if encountered, means the destruction of the earth.

---

[1] This prophesy has recently (1917) been strikingly confirmed by Dr. W. W. Campbell, Director of Lick Observatory who, in explaining why there were sudden black gaps or "holes" in the giant star clusters around which there was "a high density of star distribution right up to the sharply defined edges of the holes and yet leave the holes empty of stars," stated in his remarks on the Nebulae in the American Museum of Natural History, that "he was inclined to assume with Barnard and others, that the stars are actually there and that they are invisible because *invisible materials between us and the stars* are absorbing or hiding the light which the stars are trying to send us".... The so-called new stars afford interesting evidence on this point. *These are stars which suddenly flash out at points where previously no stars were known to exist.* . . . a temporary star is seemingly best explained on the theory that a *dark or relatively dark star* travelling rapidly through space has met with resistance."

Our System Astray:

Astronomer Serviss is quoted as saying that the earth and this whole solar system has gone astray and is trailing off away from its path around the great sun Alcyone in the Pleiades, toward the constellation Andromeda in the Milky Way. These are but astronomical confirmations of the fact that we have entered the sixth sub-race, and that the hosts are rapidly gathering for the great Battle of Armageddon.

The Redeemer Planet:

The earth is being driven through space in this new direction by the character of the thought-force of its collective humanity. But there is another planet, not yet recognized by science, which is a bright planet—the Redeemer—to be drawn into whose aura means salvation. These two planets may be called the camping grounds of the opposing forces, with the earth between as the battleground.

The Real Battle:

But back of and within the outer cause, as the propelling power, will be the preponderating force of good or evil thoughts engendered by humanity. Therefore *the real battle* is to be fought on the mental and astral planes with thoughts and psychic forces, good and bad, as weapons, and later will be reflected and precipitated on and in the earth. Hence all advanced students, who consciously determine to make Love, Brotherhood, Purity and Peace their standards of life, should enroll themselves among the Hosts of the Lord and become Soldiers of the Cross.

Baptism of Fire:

The earth and humanity are purified alternately by water and by fire, and both are now passing through a baptism of fire. Every soldier in the armies, as well as every munition maker and helper or other worker behind the lines, is helping the Great Law to bring this purifying process into manifestation. Hence each one is a servant of the Divine Flame and is helping to work out *a cosmic event* in the evolution of mankind, whether he or she knows it or not.

The Dragon:

The Dragon of the text quoted at the head of this chapter symbolizes the synthesis of the world's perverted thoughts of sex and is commonly called the Devil. The three unclean spirits like frogs which come from his mouth symbolize the three great expressions of the dragon-force, *i.e.*, (*a*) sex impurity, suppression and perversion; (*b*) the creation of disease by such perversion, and (*c*) extreme cruelty, frightfulness and insanity or psychic obsession resulting from astral entities—or individual Dwellers on the Threshold—utilizing sensitive but negative victims through which they can satisfy their desires.[1]

The Beast:

The Beast is a symbol of Mammon or greed, expressing through the Money Power. The three evil spirits issuing from his mouth comprise all the miseries and sorrows that arise as a result of greed and injustice in their threefold expressions of (*a*) wars, prosecuted for territorial or commercial expansion, stimulated and financed by the Money Power; (*b*) poverty, re-

---

[1] For full details as to the effects of obsession and their prevention or cure see *Realms of the Living Dead*, Curtiss.

sulting from the unjust distribution of wealth, which distribution is controlled by the Money Power; and (c) all the train of evils resulting from bodily and industrial slavery.

The False Prophet:

The False Prophet symbolizes all the false teachings which have been given out in the name of religion or spiritual teaching to justify and uphold both the Dragon and the Beast, but which have misled humanity and held it back from manifesting Peace, Love and Brotherhood. From his mouth come forth the three frogs of (a) materialized religion, priestcraft and temporal power and world dominion; (b) spiritual pride; and (c) intolerance and its hand-maiden, religious persecution.

King Desire:

This conflict of pride, intolerance, and persecution did not die out with the Inquisition, but is still active today. It is now directed not so much against the physical bodies of its victims, but is carried on mentally and psychically through the slanders, scandal and malicious misrepresentation carried on—especially against religious teachers—through various publications and commonly called "brutal journalism." All these factors, as the passage quoted plainly tells us, work for King Desire and his allies and their cohorts.

Carnal Weapons:

One of the first rules impressed upon the spiritual aspirant is that to attain at-one-ment by the path of Love and Purity he must lay down all carnal weapons. Jesus emphasized this rule when He said to Peter: "Put up again thy sword into his place: for all they that take the sword shall perish with the sword."[1] Yet we find the disciple spoken of as a Soldier of the Cross and commanded to array himself as a fighting factor in the world's salvation. Jesus also said: "I came not to send peace, but a sword."[2]

Plane of Causes:

Behind this paradox lies a great truth, the understanding of which is necessary ere any decided conscious advance in the spiritual unfoldment of either the individual or the Race can take place, *i.e.*, the conquering must take place

---
[1] *Matthew*, xxvi, 52.
[2] *Matthew*, x. 34.

on the plane where the causes are engendered, and the weapons are Love and Purity.

Transmute Evil:

This means that thoughts and prayers of Love and Purity must be sent out in such numbers *and with such positive spiritual force* that they will surround and transmute the impure and antagonistic forces, following the same tactics as the white warrior cells (phagocytes) of the blood use in meeting an invasion of disease germs; *i.e.*, not deny the evil, but surround and transmute the evil into Good.

Control Your Thoughts:

The Voice of the Silence tells us: "Strive with thy thoughts unclean before they overpower thee. Use them as they will thee, for if thou sparest them and they take root and grow, know well these thoughts will overpower and kill thee."[1] If you find them persistently clinging to you, send out an army of pure and loving thoughts to absorb and transmute them.

Moral Epidemics:

Science recognizes the fact that, during epidemics of disease, the mere thinking and talk-

---
[1] Blavatsky, p.12.

ing about the disease will make negative persons more susceptible to it. This does not mean that all disease is merely mental, but that by negative thoughts you open a door in your aura through which the disease can enter. This effect is still more evident in moral epidemics and in the epidemics of war-thoughts which sweep over nations.

Carnal Thoughts:

Therefore the spiritual aspirant, while fighting steadfastly for Justice and Righteousness, should lay down all carnal thoughts of hatred and revenge or he will surely "perish by the sword," overcome by the hosts of evil thought-forms he has drawn into his aura.

Karmic Readjustment:

Applied to warring nations this principle indicates that we should not waste time and force in specifically directing our prayers and thought forces to the European nations that they shall cease fighting, for they are acting under the tremendous urge of long pent-up karmic readjustment *which must take place*, and cannot respond to our prayers until after that karmic readjustment has been worked out. As well might we sit down and pray that a dirty room might be swept and cleaned without any action on our part. The result can be accomplished only by the power of the housemaid's broom.

Efficacious Prayer:

There is only one efficacious way to pray for peace and that is to pray that the Will of the Father shall be done on earth—even as it is in heaven—through those who can understand, respond to and execute that Will. That Divine Will is Love, first, last and all the time. And having prayed thus believe and know that this Divine Love is back of the entire world of manifestation, and that it is ever working to bring about the reign of universal Love, Peace and Harmony, even though it be necessary to sweep from its path all that opposes that reign.

Race Accumulations:

The terrible conditions which prevail today are not the Will of the Father, but *are the creations of man*; the result of his *resistance and opposition* to the Divine Will; the creations of unbrotherliness, ambition, selfishness, and greed, not altogether on the part of those instrumental in precipitating and now participating in the present conflict, but the accumulation of selfishness and greed of the Race, all of which must come up for adjustment now at the close of the cycle of the fifth sub-race or the end of the old dispensation, just as the rash must come out in measles, scarlet fever, etc., ere the real healing can begin.

Peace and Righteousness:

Therefore while you pray that these days be shortened, know that Peace and Righteousness *must first come in the hearts of the people of all the nations involved* and of the whole world.

Curse of Militarism:

Try not to think of individuals except in compassion, knowing that the Great Law will adjust their conditions in its own good time. Those who are dying for their ideals, even though those ideals be but of local patriotism and loyalty to an earthly ruler, are in a measure redeemers for the Race; for they are dying that the Race may be purged from the war-thought, the war-ideal and *the curse of militarism*. Hence in the next incarnation they will receive the just reward for their sacrifice.

Spiritual Compensation:

By their suffering and dying they have brought the world to a greater realization of the utter folly and *needlessness of war* if the Divine Will were followed. By their sacrifice they have wiped out much of the individual and racial Karma and will receive their compensation by being enabled to incarnate the next time very quickly, and under far more advanced conditions of civilization than they could have experienced had they remained a few years longer in the present life.

Federation of Nations:

Send your forces of Love, Peace and Brotherhood into the higher realms where they will aggregate into a mighty force which shall swallow up all future thoughts of national selfishness and aggrandizement, and be a powerful factor in forming a Federation of European Nations on the grounds of common humanity and brotherhood. This shall make it impossible for the ambitions or passions of a few to plunge nations into bloody and needless conflicts, and shall be an important factor in preparing for the coming of the Avatar.

A Super-Government:

Such a Federation of Nations would function through a Senate of 12 delegates and a House composed of representatives of all nations and peoples. This would constitute a Super-government which would have jurisdiction over all international affairs.

Enforcement:

Because of the innate selfishness of the spiritually unevolved masses, the decrees of the Federation would need to be enforced by army, navy and aerial forces contributed from the armed forces (say $1/10$) of all member nations, and financed by them.

Internal Independence:

Thus every nation and people would be independent and under the rule of whatever type of government they might choose for their internal national life, but subject to the decrees of the Federation in all matters affecting international relations. Each government would adopt and enforce a Bill of Rights adopted by the Federation, corresponding to that of the United States.

Astral Commotion:

All persons who are sensitive have realized for some time that there is a terrible commotion in the mental and astral worlds which is now intensified by the physical conflict going on in Europe, and also by the thousands of Souls suddenly thrown out of incarnation, many of whom carry with them all the excitement, antagonism and hatred which animated them as they fought.[1]

Dying in Hatred:

Those who die with hatred in their hearts and who remain unchanged in the after-life, while consciously opposing the reign of Righteousness will remain out of incarnation for a long, long cycle; in fact, until the Race has learned how to deal with them.

Emotional Control:

This composite force is like a tension or steady pressure upon all humanity, tending to make all persons more irritable and excited. Therefore it is the duty of every advanced student to take special pains to see that he does not make an opening in his aura through which

---

[1] For a full explanation of all after-death conditions see *Realms of the Living Dead*, Curtiss.

such forces can manifest by giving way to impatience, irritation and emotion or to partisanship, race and class antagonism.

Become Centers of Peace:

Instead he should consciously strive to *make himself a center* from and through which the constructive forces of Peace, Harmony, Love and Brotherhood can radiate in his family and immediate environment and on out into all the world.

Vitalized Thoughts:

Arrayed against the hosts of evil stand the thought-creations of Love, Harmony, Justice, Righteousness, Purity and upliftment of the Race sent out in a steady stream by the Lodge of Masters and by all Great Teachers since the world began, as well as by all who have been able to think *vitalized* thoughts of Love and Purity, Harmony and Brotherhood. All humanity have added and are still adding their quota to one side or the other.

Array Yourself:

It is the destiny of this fifth sub-race to see the beginning of this great and decisive battle between Good and evil or, to be more explicit, between Purity and impurity, Unselfishness and selfishness. Hence it is time that all who desire the salvation of the Race and the planet should awaken to the grave conditions we have outlined herein, and determinately array themselves on the side of Good by sending their individual, pure and vital love force to swell the Hosts of the Lord.

Loving Thoughts:

For you cannot say a loving word or do a loving deed, even to an animal, without having a loving thought behind it. And every loving and peaceful thought adds strength to the Army of the Good. As the Christ says: "Inasmuch as ye have done it unto one of the least of these my brethren, ye have done it unto me."

Hosts of the Lord:

The pure Hosts of the Lord are mustered in serried ranks according to natural law and order, while the forces of evil, being a perversion of nature and abnormal, are not organized in the astral world except into individual bands loosely held together only by self-interest, and ready at any moment to turn upon one another.

Power of Organization:

A well-known principle of warfare is that a small but well-organized army can overcome a much larger force that is unorganized. And as evil and impure forces are usually sent out by haphazard impulse they may be compared to an unorganized mob, while thoughts of Good, because they require will and effort, are consciously created, and can be gathered together by the Masters and formed into a well-drilled, well-disciplined and well-officered army, always in good fighting condition. Good is stronger than evil because it is constructive and immortal and works in harmony with the Great Law.

The Masters' Help:

The Masters of the Great White Lodge,[1] although few in numbers as compared with the multitudes of humanity, are, nevertheless, able to engender and consciously use a far greater degree of creative force on the side of Purity, Peace, Love and Brotherhood. But even They must work with the Law as Karma and may not forcibly prevent a Race or sub-race from experiencing its karmic retribution and readjustment. But Their efforts, being consciously di-

---

[1] For description see *The Voice of Isis*, Curtiss, 53, 187.

rected and wisely applied, weigh heavily in the scale.

Their Inspiration:

They do not act on the physical plane, however, except through Their disciples and those who respond to Their inspiring currents of force; hence Their great need today of those who will consciously make themselves centers of Peace, Purity, Harmony and Love and be more or less conscious instruments through which They can work. They are the directing force, comparable to the officers of an army, but the disciples must consciously become willing volunteers who shall compose the great body of fighting units which the Masters shall train and direct

Army of the Lord:

Therefore, instead of devoting all your efforts toward unfolding your faculties and developing your personality, set to work earnestly and consciously to create warriors for the Army of the Lord to the end that not only the Race but the planet itself, shall be saved from destruction.

(Released May, 1909.
Revised Sept. 30, 1914 and Sept. 15, 1917.)

CHAPTER VIII

A WORLD-WIDE CALL TO PRAYER[1]

"The effectual fervent prayer of a righteous man availeth much."
James, v, 16.

"Except those days should be shortened, there should no flesh be saved: but *for the elects sake those days shall be shortened.*"
St. Matthew, xxiv, 23.

"Prayer is a channel leading to the attainment of a fixed purpose. To pray for ourselves, is, if rightly understood, merely recognizing the inflow of Divine Love and striving to make a place for and direct it. To ask for guidance is but to take hold of the Power of Divinity as a little child grasps its father's hand."
Letters from the Teacher, Curtiss, 104-5.

The Call:

The Universal Religious Foundation calls to its students and followers in all lands, and to *all lovers of Truth, Justice and Righteousness*, to join with it at noon each day in sending up a united prayer for the success of the Allied cause.

Divine Instruments:

It is not that we are asking the powers of Divinity to aid us in killing our fellow-men, but

---
[1] Released August 7th, 1917.

to help us overcome the resistance of certain *leaders* of men to the reign of Justice and Righteousness, no matter how harsh the means required, that we may be the instruments of the Divine in bringing about the reign of Peace, Love and Harmony throughout the world.

Mass Prayer:

The concentration of the minds and hearts of thousands of advanced students in many lands who understand the power and reality of the currents of force generated by thought, aspiration, love and *the will for righteousness*, will cause such an outpouring of creative thought- and love-force that it shall rise like incense into the higher realms and rain down upon the hearts and minds of humanity with such quickening power as to fructify every mind capable of grasping and responding to the ideas which the Prayer embodies and vivifying them into action.

Prayer for the Allied Cause

O Thou loving and helpful Master Jesus![1] Thou who, standing at the right hand of the Father, seest the sorrows and afflictions of Thy children, help them to pass through the purify-

---

[1] As to the use of Jesus' name see page 135.

ing fires of suffering and sacrifice with humility, unselfishness and sanity.

As we fight that Right and Justice may prevail, help us to realize and use the Power of Righteousness that is ever present with us.

Help us to recognize through Thee the cleansing power of the divine Christ-force, that we may have a vital realization of our duty in helping to shorten these days and make thy Love and Justice prevail upon earth, even as it does in heaven.

Help us to recognize that Thy Day of Reckoning has come; the day when a national ambition that would enslave the world; when cruelty and deceitful craftiness in high places; when frightfulness on land and sea, must be swallowed up in the fierce Fires of Justice which recognize no position, rank or personality.

Pour out upon us the Love that sacrifices itself for mankind and the Power which sustains that sacrifice, that each heart may burn with ardor to achieve, and thrill with the assurance of victory for the cause of Democracy, Freedom and the Regeneration of the earth.

Grant that the Allied Nations may be so united in heart and mind and so animated by the love of mankind that the life-force of na-

tional solidarity shall fill the body of each nation full to overflowing with Courage, Sanity, Devotion and Self-sacrifice, that the victory we know must come shall be speedy and shall be a victory of the Christ over all opposition to His reign. In the name of the Living Christ we ask that these days be shortened. Amen.

Christians' Opportunity:

May the illuminating power which such a Prayer generates rouse the Christian nations to a realization of the great opportunity that confronts them, that they may rise in their strength and might as Apostles of Freedom or go down in history disgraced forever.

Ideals of Lincoln and Grant:

May their young men be filled with the Spirit of Patriotism, Justice and indomitable Courage which nothing can daunt; with the spirit which cannot see defeat, looking ever at the vision of victory, even amidst want and suffering; that they may be filled with that simple trust in the power of a just cause ever held by Abraham Lincoln, and be animated by the same tenacity of purpose that brought victory to U. S. Grant.

Shorten the Days:

In the description of those days through which the planet is now passing; it is written that "Except those days should be shortened, there should no flesh be saved: but *for the elect's sake those days shall be shortened.*" Who are the elect for whose sake these days of tribulation and retribution shall be shortened? They are those Souls who while recognizing the terrible karmic conditions through which humanity and the globe is passing, nevertheless bravely give of all they have—their loved ones, their treasure, their help in every way—with the realization that there is a power given them to shorten these days.

Heart Sympathy:

What does this mean? for it has a mighty mystic power. It is the power of your prayers, of your interest, of your full comprehension of that which is transpiring, and of your heart sympathy with those who are marching forth to lay down their lives for you and yours.

Spirit of the Race:

This great conflict is drawing together thousands of young men who have no comprehension of the seriousness of life, of the frightfulness of war and the awfulness of the things they will have to face. But in even these unawakened ones is the Spirit of the Race which in spite of all will make them give a good account of themselves.

Gaily Marching:

Thousands are marching out young and gay and trifling, with no thought of life as a serious problem, who will come back appalled with the terrors they have passed through, with all their gaiety and joyfulness plucked from their breasts by the iron hand of war.[1]

The Saddened Ones:

These are the ones who especially need our prayers and our understanding sympathy. For this is a class quite apart from those who give their lives, and from those who return wounded and crippled, and it is these saddened and stricken ones who will help make the foundations on which the new civilization must be built, be it one of law, peace and harmony or one of lawlessness or ruthless tyranny.

---

[1] Later fulfilled by those who returned wounded, shell-shocked or embittered.

The Lawless:

Others will come back filled with revenge, callous to suffering, crying out for retaliation without pity. These, too, will be among those who will rehabilitate our country. We do not want a land filled with pitilessness, cruelty and revenge. We do not want a land filled with the insanity of war. Neither do we want to go through another Inquisition nor another reign of the Puritans with their cold, joyless, unsympathetic bigotry. *Yet it is possible for all these things to come again.*

Pity, Not Revenge:

Men's hearts have existed without pity in past ages and those days may come again. Therefore hold over the world the vision of the reign of Peace, Righteousness and Sanity. Pray that our sons shall not awaken from their ignorance to become hard-hearted and revengeful. Pray that all nations shall learn out of their suffering that revenge is not the way to readjust the conditions left after the war.

Slackers:

Could you see your homes devastated, the soil of your home-land soaked with blood and your children starving, as thousands in Europe are forced to see today, and stand idly by with the pacifists and slackers? Even if the world were to end, if that meant the end of war, it would be welcome to many. But it cannot be yet.

Awaken the Elect:

There are two full Races, each with their seven sub-races, nations and tribes, yet to have their day of manifestation before the great Day of Rest. Therefore it is the duty of all the awakened to elect themselves to be the shortners of these terrible days.

Understand the Significance:

This can be done not only by letting our soldiers march forth and join hand and heart with the Allies who are making such great sacrifices—not only the men on the battlefields, but also the women at home who with the courage of willing sacrifice and thankful sorrow give the bravest and best of their sons—to achieve a noble end, but also by an *understanding of the significance* of the events of these days and those to follow, and unceasing prayer that the days be shortened.

Pray for Kindness:

Pray not only that young lives may be saved, but that their sanity, kindness of heart and love may be preserved; for they will be the ones who will return and make the laws of all the lands in the future.

Powers of Darkness:

Remember that we fight not merely against men and conditions, but against the principalities and powers of darkness which seek to push this planet out of its path that it may fail and cease to be.[1] And if they fail in one effort it is easy for them to make another unless vanquished by the Hosts of the Lord whom we invoke through prayer.

Do Your Bit:

You are not "doing your bit" if you merely go about your "business as usual" and forget to pray. Let your prayers go up unceasingly that Wisdom, Love and Righteousness may prevail; that the world may be cleansed and prepared to start the New Day purged from evil.

---

[1] See page 114.

Separate Prayers for Germany:

The fact that we do not include Germany and her allies in this Prayer—who, because she is the sheep which has gone astray and hence needs our separate prayers more than the ninety and nine who have remained within the fold—may seem to some that we are not fulfilling the law of the Christ which says, "Love your enemies, do good to them which hate you. Bless them that curse you, and pray for them which despitefully use you."

Prayer Against Compulsion:

We admit the law and endeavor to follow it, but we are convinced that while *the German people* need our love and our prayers, yet since her *leaders* have permitted her to become the avenue through which all the evils we are praying to overcome have been permitted to manifest on earth, we must pray for the success of all those forces which are fighting to overcome these evils and sweep from the earth those influences which have *deliberately brought this terrible war* upon mankind, and which seek to prolong it that they may impose their will upon the nations of the world to their enslavement.

Germany's Awakening:

We send out this prayer because we believe that *America* and the Allies are fighting for Right and Justice, yet *we pray just as sincerely* that Germany may awaken[1] to a realization of her shortcomings and crimes, and the people of Germany to their duty to uphold Truth, Justice and Righteousness, Freedom and Self-government against the whims' and passions of an irresponsible autocracy. Yet the place of a petition for Germany is not in the present Prayer, for this is a special prayer for the success of those forces which are engaged in sweeping from the world militarism and autocracy, a necessary condition for the New Age upon which we are entering.

A Master of Masters:

In using the name of Jesus we are not merely praying to a man who lived nearly two thousand years ago, but we consciously recognize Him as the Great Master of Masters who is at the head of the divine Healing Hierarchy, ever ready to answer such a call and pour out His forces upon

---

[1] Germany's awakening resulted in the "loss of morale" for war and the call for an armistice.

us, not to relieve us from our responsibility for the sin and suffering we have created, but to instil into each heart something of His own power both of seeing the beauty of Righteousness and Justice, and the strength to establish the same upon earth.

The Name of Jesus:

The name of Jesus has great power and potency, for it stands for the Man who has conquered, who is our example, who is God. For we also can conquer if we open our hearts to the inflow of the Christ-force.

Power of the Christ:

Such a call sent up from the united hearts of our many, many students in all lands, and of our sympathizing friends, who know how to pray, *i.e.*, who know that we are not asking to have someone else do something for us, but that the Power of the Christ shall so fill us that we may accomplish for ourselves, will bless every man in all the ranks and enable them to do all that Jesus has promised could be accomplished through the same Spirit of the Christ that made Him one with the Father.

Our Realization:

Only such a call can pierce the earth-born clouds *created by man's misconception* and misunderstanding which hide the earthly from the Divine, and open his consciousness to the realization that the Divine is also in him. To the degree that we lay our lives and our loves, our goods and our gains upon the altar of sacrifice that the world may be cleansed from evil, so shall it be.

Effect of Prayer:

If your eyes could be opened to see the effect the repetition of this Prayer produces in the higher realms and the forces it brings to your aid, your faith would be strengthened and your heart assured. Especially is it effective when sent up from the hearts of many persons at the same time or successively a few at a time, as will be the case if every student repeats it at 12 o'clock noon on each day.

Always Noon Somewhere:

As it is noon at some part of the globe all the time, and as our pupils extend around the world, there will be a ceaseless repetition of this prayer throughout the twenty-four hours of the day. We therefore expect great power to result from this continuous Day of Prayer.

Coöperation Needed:

We ask all our students, and all the friends who will cooperate with us, to pin this announcement up where it will be called to their attention daily and to meditate upon it and repeat it daily *until the war is over and harmonious conditions established*. If it is not committed to memory it should be copied and carried in the pocket so that no matter where they are or what they may be doing outwardly they will have it at hand to read and repeat.

Meditation:

If possible its repetition should be followed by a period of silence and meditation during which the spiritual power invoked should be seen pouring down upon America and the Allies and their forces, flooding all with the light of spiritual understanding and the courage of religious conviction.

Pray Daily:

Repeat the Prayer aloud daily and then sit in silence and realize its potency for the triumph of Justice and Righteousness. Keep on doing this daily until the war is over and peace is restored to all nations.

Shorten These Days:

If you lift up your hearts in prayer unceasing you have it in your power to stop this war. If you raise your hands in supplication day after day and night after night, never forgetting the terror the world is passing through and the power of the Christ to conquer all conditions when truly invoked, *these days shall be shortened.* But you must elect yourselves to be the shorteners of these days.

Do Not Hinder:

Do not give aid or sympathy to those who would hinder America from doing her part, lest America have to stand in the Day of Judgment with head bowed in shame because she was too slow in striking a blow for Freedom and Civilization.

Sanity Needed:

Pray not only for peace, but for sanity. It is sanity that is needed. For the world is going mad, one class ignoring the suffering of another class; one class mad with sudden wealth, gaiety and frivolity, another class mad with poverty, sacrifice, suffering and horror.

Keep Poised:

Keep your minds balanced and poised and help to keep others from going to extremes. Pray for the sanity and normal balance of the world. Talk it. Preach it. Pray for it.

Hold Fast:

Hold fast to normal balance first in our own country and then in the countries which are fighting your battles, then for all who are the victims of this madness that is obsessing the world.

(This call to a daily noon-tide Prayer for the Allies was sent throughout the world by the Order of Christian Mystics on August 7, 1917. The special day to inaugurate its universal repetition was set for September 9, 1917, at which time a special service was held at the Headquarters of the Order then in Philadelphia. Since that time the idea has rapidly gained ground and churches of all denominations in many cities have inaugurated similar services, thus showing that the inspiration of the idea is finding response in every heart and mind attuned to it.

All who read this are urged, not only to repeat the Prayer daily, but to present the subject to the religious leaders of their community and endeavor to have some kind of Noon Prayer Service for the Allies inaugurated and continued until the war is over and conditions of peace are firmly established. (Aug. 7, 1917)

CHAPTER IX

A PRAYER FOR WORLD HARMONY[1]

"Prayer is an aspiration of the Soul toward the Divine. It may also be a request, not for creature comforts or physical things, but for spiritual food, love, light, courage, protection and help. In fact, prayer creates a magnetic line of force which unites you with the supply. . . . The repetition of this prayer is like a projectile fired through the earth's atmosphere creating a passage through which the One Life must necessarily flow."
The Voice of Isis, Curtiss, 347, 343.

"Men's hearts failing them for fear, and for looking after those things which are coming on the earth. . . . And when these things begin to come to pass, then look up, and lift up your heads; for your redemption draweth nigh."
St. Luke, xxi, 26, 28.

Overhanging Clouds:

The remarkable and world-wide acclaim and favorable response which has been accorded to President Roosevelt's recent "Three Point Peace Plan," even by Herr Hitler, the Dictator of Germany, is a splendidly encouraging sign

---
[1] Released in June 1933.

that the fifty-four nations to whom it was sent really desire permanent peace. The constructive currents of international harmony thus generated and the prospect that the United States will end its traditional policy of isolation, will do much to draw the nations closer together and help to neutralize the selfish and antagonistic currents formerly generated by intense nationalism. But there is still a tremendous amount of old Karma that was not worked out and adjusted by the World War and subsequent events. It is this tremendous black cloud of Karma which is hanging over mankind which we are so anxious to see dissipated *before it is precipitated* into physical expression.

A Call to Prayer:

The favorable response to President Roosevelt's proposals offers an open door through which the leaders and also the hearts of the nations can be reached. We therefore earnestly ask that the wave of international amity thus begun shall be reinforced, maintained continuously and expanded by our students throughout the world—for above all others they should be able to grasp the vital significance of the opportunity and understand the power of organized prayer—again taking up *The Prayer for World Harmony* whose repetition proved so effective in former years (1917 and 1922), and repeating it daily during their periods of meditation. For this is necessary if we desire the present wave of peace and international amity to be more than temporary, and if we are to prevent the karmic storm clouds now hovering over mankind from being precipitated upon the earth plane.

Destruction Menaces:

As the Master told us some time ago:[1] "The time has come when the power of cooperation and harmony among nations; when real Brotherhood and Divine Love must and shall rule and the mind and its ambitions shall obey; when Divine Love shall be dominant; when the illumined mind shall be Its servant and eager to do Its will. The powers of destruction *are preparing to manifest in a tremendous way* on the Earth's surface. Therefore, *special efforts must be put forth to radiate* Peace, Harmony and Brotherhood in such floods of radiant energy that it shall neutralize the evil and minimize the destructive character of the coming

---
[1] *Coming World Changes*, Curtiss, 108-118.

changes. If this great lesson can be really learned and manifested and put into daily practice by even a small portion of humanity, the whole world can pass through the coming great crossing over the Earth's forces and really enter the Aquarian Age quickly and without one-half the catastrophes and destruction that will be absolutely necessary if this great lesson remains unlearned.

Power of Conscious Prayer:

"With the thought clearly held in mind that *these days shall be shortened* we can work toward that definite end. *Realize that prayers thus consciously and understandingly used* are not mere sequences of pious words, but are a definite means of invoking Spiritual Fire and providing channels through which it can manifest in humanity. . . . No need to ask God to save humanity from the results of its own creating. *It is humanity itself that must save itself through the manifestation of its God-powers* which are always ready at hand to be invoked and used *by those who will make the effort*, else humanity could never gain self-mastery. . . . *Conditions never right themselves*, they are righted only through the *definite constructive action* of certain persons or groups of persons who understand and unite to work wisely toward definite ends.

Positive Effort Needed:

"The whole world is today passing through a dense smothering cloud of karmic dust which has accumulated through the ages of wrong thinking and acting, wrong conceptions of the *Law of Life.* And, alas, many are letting this dust so blind the eyes of their understanding that they believe that only through extreme selfishness, retaliation and revenge can they end their injustice and suffering and let peace, brotherhood, justice and prosperity reign. This idea is being so systematically propagated among the unthinking masses that *unless some positive effort is made* by those who know the *Law of Life*—harmony and cooperation—those who see and feel and know that all such separative and destructive ideas will only result in a prolongation of the same conditions from which mankind has suffered so long, together with all those who desire better conditions, all united in *a persistent effort* to make a firm stand on *the principles of harmony and interdependence*, which we see exemplified among the various organs of our bodies, *the world is destined to rehearse once more*[1] the terrible drama of destruction, death and suffering unspeakable which it has already passed through in so many previous cyclic periods of revolution inaugurated in the name of freedom and reform. . . .

The First to Help:

"The first to work definitely with the Spiritual Powers which are seeking to lift up the gates of ignorance and inculcate the constructive principles of the *Law of Life* should be those advanced students whose consciousness can grasp and realize this Law and its applications, as they have been set forth in our Cosmic Soul Science in the wide scope and variety of our philosophical and spiritual books and teachings. . . .

Combat Wrong Principles:

"Firstly, we must systematically spread the idea that it is *wrong principles and rules of life* we are to combat, *not persons or peoples or races*. . . . We must also continually spread the idea that force, coercion, revenge, hatred, cruelty, even the repetition of and *clinging to*

---

[1] This prophecy is now fulfilled in 1939.

the memory of wrongs we have suffered, are destructive forces which can only *add to and never heal* the wounds from which all the world is groaning today. . . .

Prayer an Innate Instinct:

"Prayer is an innate instinct in the human Soul, and common alike to the savage and the most cultured and intellectual of mankind. It is, therefore, as natural for man to pray—especially in times of crisis which transcend the power of man to cope with—as to breathe or think.

Not Selfish Prayer:

"In this case we are asking our readers to unite in prayer, not because they have been frightened at the prospect. . . . not to save their own lives or even their own Souls, but to help generate such a constructive spiritual power as will counteract the evil and destructive forces and thus help to save humanity from the suffering through which it must pass if the destructive forces are not neutralized. . . .

Currents Generated:

"The uniting of thousands of hearts and minds to this definite end should generate a great current of dynamic spiritual force sweeping continuously around the world—for it is noon somewhere every minute of the day—which like a refreshing breeze should cool the heat of conflicting interests and blow off the karmic dust of the past which is settling upon and blinding individuals and nations to the *Law of Life*—harmony and cooperation. Thus shall we be of practical psychological help in opening wide "the everlasting doors" and preparing for the quick coming of the King of Glory, not only into our own hearts and lives, but into the lives of nations and humanity as a whole.

Unite on Principles:

"Remember that the battle which is still raging in the world is *a battle of principles*, and that the *Law of Life* must ultimately prevail. But it will prevail only after terrible calamities and renewed suffering to individuals, classes and nations *unless they unite* to lift up their gates and permit the King of Glory to come in and help them transmute the clouds of karmic dust and inharmony into peace, brotherhood and cooperation. Only as men open their hearts to Him can He enter in and bring true peace.

Visualize the Radiance:

"See the radiance which this Prayer invokes, dispelling the clouds of inharmony as the Sun dispels the fog, and stimulating the growth of the good in each heart as the Sun stimulates the growth of the sprout when the fog has been dispelled and the Sun can carry on its constructive work.

Prayer for World Harmony

Glory and honor and worship be unto Thee, O Lord Christ, Thou who art the Life and Light of all mankind!

Thou are the King of Glory, to whom all the peoples of the Earth should give joyful allegiance and service.

Inspire mankind with a realization of true Brotherhood.

Teach us the wisdom of peace, harmony and cooperation.

Breathe into our hearts the understanding that only as we see ourselves as parts of the one body of humanity can peace, harmony, success and plenty descend upon us.

Help us to conquer all manifestations of inharmony and evil in ourselves and in the world.

May all persons and classes and nations cease their conflicts, and unselfishly strive for peace and good-will, that the days of tribulation may be shortened.

Bless us all with the Radiance of Thy divine Love and Wisdom, that we may ever worship Thee in the beauty of holiness.

In the name of the Living Christ we ask it. Amen.

The Day of Preparation:

"This is the day given you to prepare. Cry it from the housetops *to those who know and can understand*. The Day is at hand. Shall it be a day of great peace, of wonderful illumination? A majority of Christ-illumined ones? Or shall it be another cycle of darkness more terrible than any that has passed into the world's history? For much has been given to mankind and much will be required. Even to the worldly ones much has been given: great understanding has been poured forth. Out of mighty tribulation much is sensed and comprehended, hence much is required. . . .

A Cycle of Darkness:

"If this generation fails, then the whole system must pass once more down into the *darkness from which it has so laboriously emerged. A blank ignorance will oppress humanity. Cruelty and a deliberate turning from the Light will wipe out all that civilisation has attained. Chaos will reign among people. Art and literature will be destroyed and forgotten. Great inventions that are only waiting for proper conditions to come forth for the benefit of humanity will be smothered in birth.*

Look and Decide:

"Look on the two pictures and *decide where you stand*. It is as though you were called to follow the colors. What will *you* do to help save civilization? Remember it is not yourself that you must help save, but our Christian civilization.

Worry and Fear Retard:

"Worry and fear only add to the world's misery, while every happy, courageous heart sows seeds of happiness and trust and courage in the hearts of others. Those who elect to help shorten these days should send out their aspiration, love and compassion in constant prayer, that it may dispell men's fears and teach them to trust utterly in God's guidance.

Cooperate in Prayer:

"Therefore, we ask all who will to use some such prayer as our *Prayer for World Harmony* morning, noon and night, and *spread this idea as widely as possible* that its vibrations may affect and inspire the hearts of mankind, and *particularly the leaders of nations*. The use of this Prayer or mantram will not only have a psychological effect, according to the mental and spiritual force we put into it, but it will also form an avenue in the body of humanity for the manifestation of the hierarchies of Divine Ones who have charge of the ushering in of the coming New Age through which They can reach the minds and hearts of men.

Not Vain Repetition:

"Remember that it is not merely repeating the words that brings the power, but repeating them with all the aspiration and spiritual power implanted in us by the Eternal Being in the beginning. It is not lip-service the Holy Ones ask of us, but sincere effort and *understanding prayer*.

Meditate and Visualize:

"Pause after each sentence and meditate upon it, visualizing its radiance going out to all mankind, consuming all evil and stimulating all good. For it is only through softening the hearts of mankind, through the spread of the warmth of Divine Love and the power of the Living Christ, that *the evil can be overcome and these days can be shortened."*

Watch and Expect Results:

"Watch for the beginning of the changes. Watch and wait and believe in the power of the Christ. Be undaunted and true of heart. Be strong and loving and faithful, not weak, fearful and vacillating. Be not turned aside by earthly and materialistic conceptions of the *Law of Life*. Bow not the knee to Baal, but stand firm and apart in the Temple of Silence[1] and recognize your great opportunities to spread the Light of Truth. Be not dismayed at any trial or disaster.

Rest in Confidence:

"Rest in peace and blessing while opposition threatens you and cries out curses upon God and man. Pray for peace and plenty while famine stalks through the land. Pray for peace and stability while nations clash and continents dis-

---

[1] For details see *The Temple of Silence*, Curtiss.

appear. For lo, the time is at hand when all that has been foretold shall shortly come to pass. Be ye therefore prepared. Be ye planted in the courtyard of the Temple of the Living God. Let none of these things affright or move you. Let not your hearts be troubled. Recognize your oneness with the Divine, "and lo, I am with you always, even unto the end of the world. Amen."

Will You Enlist?

"Will you enlist in this great undertaking? Will you devote your life, your love, your understanding, your all, to the solving of the greatest problem humanity has ever faced? to bring peace and harmony and co-operation out of the present-day confusion, unbrotherliness and war, that the one Divine Light may shine forth and illumine the hearts of all mankind?

CHAPTER X

THE SYMBOLOGY OF THE STARS AND STRIPES

Symbol of Attainment:

A national flag not only symbolically embodies the highest ideals of the people over whom it flies, but it also symbolizes the highest attainment and ultimate perfection of that people.

Our Key-note:

The flag of the United States of America symbolizes and foreshadows the greatest possibilities of any flag ever designed. Although there are many flags having the same colors, yet in none are they combined in a like manner. The colors of a flag are like the letters spelling a word or the notes of music forming a melody. Therefore the flag of each nation proclaims its word and sounds its key-note, hence rallies to it the elemental powers and forces belonging to its color and symbols.

Meaning of Red:

In our flag the red symbolizes the blood or life-force, the martial force, its clear bright shade representing all the higher possibilities of the courage, energy and power of Mars, the masculine force in the solar system and in humanity, as well as the intensity of love that will fight for principle.

Force of Mars:

The red of Mars is alternated at equal intervals with the white of purity, sanity, righteousness, justice and brotherhood. This proclaims to the world that we will fight if we have to, not because we seek to spill our brother's blood or for aggrandizement, but for righteousness, justice, freedom and liberty. For these must be maintained by the force of Mars if necessary, else our flag is unbalanced and the principles for which it stands are betrayed. But we should let the white so blend with the red that it will color into the light rose pink of love.

Balance:

It also indicates that war is not the governing spirit, but is blended and balanced in equal proportion with the desire for peace honorably won and maintained by the higher aspects of Mars.

Meaning of Blue:

Blue is the color of the Great Mother-force, the power which brings forth and which cherishes all that is beautiful and lovable, as well as those things which the force of Mars energizes. In other words, it represents the force of Venus or Divine Mother-love.

Our Arrangement:

No other flag has the arrangement of these two colors as found in our flag. Others have the blue, but not in one great mass like a sea of color on which the five-pointed stars are arranged side by side in harmonious order.

Power of White:

And because the white and the red are co-equal, our victories must be won as much by the powers of the white as those of the red. If there were a large field of white it would tend to symbolize peace at any price, but since it is equally balanced by the red it symbolizes peace, but peace attained and maintained if necessary by righteous war.

White Stars:

Since the five-pointed star symbolizes man,[1] the white stars, *i.e.*, the purified men and women, set in their field of blue symbolize the gathering together of all humanity into the lap of the Great Mother. They stand for the united brotherhood which holds out its arms to all mankind to come and become one of US. And if they come in love and harmony and are willing to rest in the lap of their adopted mother, each in his proper place and *ready to obey her decrees, laws and requirements*, they are welcome. But if they cannot take their places thus on the field of blue, the flag has no place for them.

The Flag Proclaims:

In its emblem this country thus proclaims to the world that is has conceived and set before its children the high ideal and glorious opportunity of becoming the leader in liberty and freedom in that it offers freely a home for all God's children, a country in which to found the New Humanity. The responsibility is great. Will we as a nation live up to it? Or through carelessness will we allow subversive activities to flourish?

---

[1] For explanation see *The Key to the Universe*, Curtiss, 181.

Our Pledge:

Each one of us should be glad that we have a flag with such a wonderful meaning, and each should study its higher, esoteric symbology; for it enables each one to say, "I belong to a new country and a new people. I will do all I can to make this country and this people all that our flag symbolizes. I will do my duty in all ways to keep the flag waving over this country, and also over the whole world in the sense of upholding the highest ideals of freedom, justice, righteousness and brotherhood!"

Patriotism:

This subject would not be complete were we to omit a word on the subject of patriotism, a subject so blatantly proclaimed by many with little realization of its inner meaning, and by others—especially a certain class of would-be students who measure everyone's corn in their own meager basket—is decried and scornfully relegated to the scrap-heap of outgrown and provincial ideas, good only for children to amuse themselves with, or who cannot grasp what they think to be the greater idea of internationalism.

Our Nation:
But since no man can live unto himself alone, any more than a Soul can be incarnate without the aid of physical parents, and since no nation can rise above the highest ideas the majority can grasp, the nation of our adoption—whether of our birth or not—in which we think, act, strive and develop, in the deeper sense is indeed our "pater" (father) to whom we owe our patriotism.

You Owe Allegiance:
And since every thought, act and endeavor of ours has sprung up in and helped to create the nation, not only are we subject to it and owe it allegiance, but we have become so inextricably woven into its national karma that failure to give it our best and to make every sacrifice for it is to be a double traitor, a traitor to our own ideals and a traitor to the country which we have helped to make what it is; for its failure is our failure, its high station our triumph and pride.

Sophistry:
Hence to say, as some of the surface thinkers do, that they owe no allegiance to their flag or

country; that one country and one flag is as good for them as another, since all are one, and their allegiance is to the brotherhood of man and to the inner command of the Spirit which alone they will recognize any obligation to, all such talk we say is but to proclaim their own shallowness and ignorance and lack of real development, and to blind themselves with sophistry.

Symbol of Ideals:

For the flag of the nation to which we have given our allegiance, our deepest thoughts and our highest ideals, and from the united thought-force of whose children we have gained our strength and success, is a symbol not alone of that nation, but a symbol as well of everything to which we have attained or striven, because the laws and conditions established by the nation to which that flag belongs are the stepping-stones upon which our own development has risen, the very incentives to our advance.

INDEX

A

Adjustment, Law of, 94.
Age, Aquarian, 33, 47; of Brotherhood, 21; Golden, 31, 94; New, 40-5; Piscean, 21; Woman's, 33.
Agnosticism, 26.
Alcyone, 109.
Allegiance, You owe, 160-1.
Allegories, 18.
Allies, interests of, 54; prayer for, 125, 140; tests of, 56.
America, 22, 30, 43, 140, 155.
Andromeda, 109.
Angels, guardian, 93; of presence, 69, 70; song of, 61-2, 72.
Antagonism, radiates, 11.
Anti-Christ, 2, 3, 8, 9, 10, 108.
Aquarius, Sign of, 43.
Arbitrator, Man the, 84-7.
Atheism, 2.
Atlanteans, 90, 101.
Atlantis, sinking of, 101.
Atoms, sloughed off, 19.
Aura, opening in, 120.
Australia, 24.
Avatar, the coming, 39, 118.

B

Babe, within, 72.
Banner, Thy, 12.
Baptism, of blood, 22; of fire, 110.
Battle, astral, 105, 110; final, 106.
Beast, the, 111.
Being, no arbitrary, 15.
Blood, baptism of, 22; of the Lamb, 47.
Blow-torch, prayer like a, 15.
Blue, meaning of, 157.
Body, spiritual, 47.
Bolshevism, 1.
Borgias, 99.
Bread, His, 45; of Life, 49.
Breath, of Life, 81.
Broadcast, forces are, 11.
Brotherhood, test of, 34.

C

Cataclysms, of illness, 42; world, 100, 106.
Chaos, possible, 157.
Chasteneth, He, 85.
Children, effect on, 71-2.
Church, Christian, 42.
Civilization, advanced, 46; Angel of, 69; definition of, 2; harmony needed, 70; the new, 131; test of, 33-4-5.
Communists, 3.
Compensation, spiritual, 116, 118.
Concentration, 14.
Condemn, none, 13.
Conditions, stable needed, 7.
Conrad, of Marburg, 104.
Consciousness, shell of, 40; spiritual, 87.
Co-operation, needed, 138.
Corridor, Polish, 1.
Corruption, sown in, 47.
Craving, Soul, 34.
Creations, of man, 8.
Creator, the reaps, 7.
Cup, His, 45.
Curses, man's, 85; removed, 88.

Cycles, close, 21.
Czarism, 30.

D

Danzig, 1.
Darkness, cycle of, 150; powers of, 9, 133.
Day-periods, 59.
Democracies, ideals of, 2.
Desire, King, 91, 112.
Despise, none, 13.
Despotism, 2, 3.
Destiny, man's, 73.
Destroyer, planet, 108.
Devil, the, 111.
Disasters, coming, 106.
Diseases, malignant, 63; world, 64.
Dragon, the, 21, 66, 80, 111.
Duty, your, 12.
Dweller, the, 93, 108, 111.
Dying, in hatred, 120.

E

Elect, the, 38, 129, 132.
Emotions, control, 120; radiate. 11: war of, 92.
England, 24.
Entities, astral, 99, 100.
Epidemics, moral, 114.
Europe, a focal point, 103.
Evil, battle of, 101; good from, 54; precipitated, 22; transmute, 114.

F

Factor, you are a, 14, 15.
Fathers, Lunar, 80-1-9; Solar, 80-1.
Fear, cast out, 4, 151.
Federation, of nations, 32, 116-18.
Fire, baptism of, 110; spiritual, 15.
Flag, ideals of our, 161; proclaims, 158.
Flame, Divine, 110.
Flattery, 99; 105.
Foundation, Universal Religious, 1, 125.
France, 23.
Freedom, spiritual, 1, 3.
Free-will, 7.

G

Generation, if fails, 151.
Germans, misled, 3; people, the, 1, 27, 55, 134; revolution, 4.
Germany, 26-7, 134-5.
Glory, King of, 148.
God, Wills of the, 39, 41; Solar, 101.
God, Sons of, 101.
Government, Super, 119.
Grain, spiritual, 49.
Guidance, Divine, 91.

H

Halifax, disaster of, 53.
Hand, time is at, 98.
Harmony, individual, 10; law of, 22.
Harvard, observatory, 108.
Hate, do not, 3; dying in, 120.
Healing, real, 19.
Helios, 80.
Hell, created, 89.
Hercules, 80.
Hermes, 75.
Herod, 60.
Hitler, 1, 28-9, 103, 141.
Horus, 80.
Hosts, of the Lord, 122.
Humanity, save, 15; the new, 107.

I

Ideal, 21.
Ideologies, war of, 37.
Ignorance, 8, 80.
Illness, cataclysms of, 92.
Incense, 14.
Inharmony, creates, 11, 12.
Initiation, 93.
Injustice, 56.
Inquisition, 42, 104-5, 131.
Inspiration, 124.
Instruments, human, 99.
Intellect, 87.
Intuition, 83-7.
Irritation, greater now, 10.
Israel, 60.

J
Jerusalem, the new, 49, 50.
Jesus, name of, 135-6.
K
Kaiser, 28-9, 103.
Karma, in Bible, 45-6; is readjustment, 44, 94, 105, 115; Lords of, 51-3; of all, 37, 142; of Church, 103; race, 102-7; of Russia, 29; unredeemed, 99; world, national, personal, 52.
Kingdoms, lower, 85.
L
Lamb, blood of the, 47.
Lancet, war a, 19.
Law, Divine, 8.
Leaders, deluded, 103; egotistical, 100; ideals of, 8.
Lemuria, 107.
Life, law of, 145-6-8, 153; waters of, 47.
Light, the, 20.
Lincoln, ideals of, 128.
Lodge, Great White, 123.
Lord, army of the, 124.
Lucifer, 66-8.
M
Magic, black and white, 101.
Man, brotherhood of, 21; sign of the Son of, 41-3.
Manas, 84.
Manifestation, basis of, 37.
Marburg, Conrad, 104.
Mars, 156.
Masses, express, 13.
Masters, 98, 123, 135.
Matter, and Spirit, 78.
Mercury, 48.
Michael, 66.
Militarism, 80, 117.
Mill, of Gods, 39, 41.
Mind, higher, 84-88; sons of, 81.
Mistakes, man's, 59.
Money- power, 111.
Moon, gods, 89.

Morale, loss of, 5, 12, 135.
Moses, 90-1.
Myth, the sun, 79, 91.
N
Nationalism, 64.
Nations, Federation of, 32, 116-17-18; sick, 19; Slavonic, 35.
Nero, 99.
New Jerusalem, the, 51.
Neutrality, 3.
O
Observatory, 108.
Obsessed, 4.
Ones, great, 51.
Operation, needed, 65.
Organization, power of, 123.
P
Pacifist, 68.
Paganism, 10.
Pater, 160.
Patriotism, 159.
Peace, centers of, 4, 121; Chapter V, 57, 68; descends, 60; God's plan, 7; pray for, 254.
Penn, William, 43.
Personality, husks of, 41.
Phagocytes, 114.
Pharoah, 91.
Pisces, age of, 21.
Pity, 3, 131.
Plan, God's, 7, 40, 73; grand, 8, 58.
Planet, dark, 108; destroyer, 108; redeemer, 109.
Poise, battles for, 19, 140.
Poland, 1.
Powers, of darkness, 9; role of, 62.
Pray, how to, 16, 17.
Prayer, for allies, 126, 140; call to, 137; is instinctive, 147; for Germany, 133; mass, 126; noon, 13, 16, 137; power of, 4, 13, 116, 126, 137, 144, 152; stop war, 12; world harmony, 141-3-9; world peace, 16.

Principalities, of air, 9.
Principles, wrong, 13, 148.
Propaganda, 9.
Prophet, the false, 112.
Psychology, law of, 20.
Python, 80

Q

Quotations from:
Campbell, Dr., 108.
Coming World Changes, 14, 143.
I Corinthians, 6.
The Eucharist, 42-5.
Genesis, 81-5.
The Great Migration, 91.
The Inner Radiance, 91.
Jeremiah, 6, 97-8-9.
The Key to the Universe, 59, 105, 157.
Letters from the Teacher, vol. i, 125.
Lévi, Éliphas, 89.
Magic, Transcendental, 18.
The Message of Aquaria, 41, 53
Micah, 57.
Realms of the Living Dead, 111, 120.
Revelation, 97.
St. James, 125.
St. Luke, 6, 141.
St Matthew, 113, 125.
The Secret Doctrine, 75-6-8, 90, 102.
The Sign Aquarius, 22, 31, 48.
The Temple of Silence, 153.
The Universal Sun Myth, 79.
The Voice of Isis, 25, 67, 81- 6, 95, 102-7, 123. 141.
The Voice of the Silence, 114.
Why Are We Here?, 33, 57.
The Zohar, 76.

R

Race, 4th, 101; 5th, 102-5; 6th, 107.
Rama, 101.
Ramayana, 101.

Rasputin, 9.
Ravana, 90, 101.
Ray, of Spirit, 16, 81-2-4.
Reactions, control, 11.
Reckoning, day of, 127.
Red, meaning of, 156.
Redemption, 86-7.
Resistance, Principle of,
Chapt vi, 75-7; cease to the Divine, 22, 62.
Respond, gladly, 30; refuse to, 21.
Responsibility, man's, 7, 11, 12.
Revolt, mental, 36.
Revolution, 4.
Rights, bill of, 119.
Roosevelt, President, 141-3.
Russia, 9, 25-9.

S

Sacrifice, 3.
Sanctuaries, 51.
Satan, 66.
Saturn, 46-7-8; 67-9.
St George, 21.
St Gregory, 75.
St Paul, 83.
Self-chosen, ones, 99.
Self-determination, 1.
Science, Cosmic Soul, 75.
Sick, nations are, 19, 64.
Sign, of Aquarius, 43; of the Son of Man, 41.
Six, number, 105.
Slackers, 131.
Smile, 12.
Song, angels', 61.
Soul, craving, 34.
Stability, essential, 6.
Stars, white, 157.
Stars and Stripes, 155.
Sun-gods, 89.
Sun Myth, 79.
Symbols, materialized, 42-5.
Sympathy, heart, 129.
Sword, perish by the, 113.

T

Teacher, the Great, 39, 40.
Tester, Saturn the, 67.
Tests, 33-4-5-8; 48.
Thinking, spiritual, 90; wrong, 43.
Thought forces, neutralize, 12, 14, 114.
Thoughts, are things, 11; carnal, 115; control, 114; fruit of, 98; power of, 61; vitalized, 121; will express, 30.
Tolerance, 37.
Traitor, 160.
Transmute, 93.
Tribulation, days of, 139.

U

Unselfishness, war develops, 32.

V

Venus, 48, 157.
Visualize, 153.

W

War, aspects of, Chapt iv, 32; a shock, 60 causes of, 8, 9; cosmic, 79; in heaven, 66, 79; last stopped, 12; last world, 8, 107; object of, 1; Mahabharatan, 90; stopped by, 4; uselessness of, 118; why, Chapt iii, 3, 18; why permitted, 18.
War, "the", Chapt vi, 75; astral, 105, 110, 140; cause of, 77.
Water, of life, 47.
Wealth, role of, 62.
Weapons, carnal, 113.
White, meaning of, 157.
Will, Divine, 8, 21, 63, 116-18; not the Father's, 7, 116.
Winds, North, 54; the four, 47, 53.
Woman, position of, 34; work of, 65, 70.

www.ingramcontent.com/pod-product-compliance
Lightning Source LLC
Chambersburg PA
CBHW071502040426
42444CB00008B/1450